# GLOBETROTTER™

## *Travel Guide*

# TENERIFE

## ROWLAND MEAD

NEW
HOLLAND

NEW HOLLAND

★★★ Highly recommended
★★ Recommended
★ See if you can

Second edition published in 2005
by New Holland Publishers (UK) Ltd
London • Cape Town • Sydney • Auckland
First published in 2002

10 9 8 7 6 5 4 3 2 1

website: www.newhollandpublishers.com

Garfield House, 86 Edgware Road
London W2 2EA
United Kingdom

80 McKenzie Street
Cape Town 8001
South Africa

14 Aquatic Drive
Frenchs Forest, NSW 2086
Australia

218 Lake Road
Northcote, Auckland
New Zealand

Distributed in the USA by
The Globe Pequot Press
Connecticut

ISBN 1 84537 072 4

Although every effort has been made to ensure that
this guide is up to date and current at time of going
to print, the Publisher accepts no responsibility or
liability for any loss, injury or inconvenience
incurred by readers or travellers using this guide.

**Publishing Manager (UK):** Simon Pooley
**Publishing Manager (SA):** Thea Grobbelaar
**DTP Cartographic Manager:** Genené Hart
**Editors:** Thea Grobbelaar, Nic Orfang
**Design and DTP:** Lellyn Creamer, Nicole Bannister
**Cartographers:** Nicole Bannister, Genené Hart
**Picture Research:** Shavonne Johannes,
Colleen Abrahams
**Consultants:** Katerina and Eric Roberts
Reproduction by Hirt & Carter (Pty) Ltd, Cape Town
Printed and bound by Times Offset (M) Sdn. Bhd.,
Malaysia

**Keep us Current**
Information in travel guides is apt to change, which
is why we regularly update our guides. We'd be
grateful to receive feedback if you've noted something we should include in our updates. If you have
new information, please share it with us by writing
to the Publishing Manager, Globetrotter, at the office
nearest to you (addresses on this page). The most
significant contribution to each new edition will
receive a free copy of the updated guide.

**Cover:** *Palm trees on the beach at Teresitas.*
**Title page:** *A traditional folk-music group.*

# CONTENTS

# 1
# Introducing Tenerife

The largest of the Canary Islands, Tenerife is also the most attractive and diverse. Dominated by the snow-capped volcano of Mount Teide, the highest mountain in Spain, the island also has pine forests, deep ravines or *barrancos*, banana plantations, towering cliffs and arid semi-desert areas reminiscent of the Sahara. Bathed by warm Atlantic waters, freshened by the trade winds and blessed by almost perpetual sun, Tenerife has been described as the 'land of eternal spring'. Little wonder that it has become a year-round tourist destination.

Tourists flock to the drier south of the island, where purpose-built resorts such as **Playa de las Américas** and **Los Cristianos** provide entertainment, nightlife, theme parks and reliable sunshine. The steady wind and impressive waves make this an ideal area for watersports such as windsurfing and sailing. Hikers, on the other hand, prefer the centre and north of Tenerife, where there is a wide network of country paths. On the north of the island stands the more sedate resort of **Puerto de la Cruz**, surrounded by old towns and luxuriant vegetation. Many visitors spend a day in the capital city and port of **Santa Cruz**. It was here that Admiral Nelson lost his arm in a naval battle.

Tenerife also has its historical towns. Just to the west of Santa Cruz is **La Laguna**, the site of the main university of the Canary Islands. Further west is **La Orotava**, with a fine collection of historical buildings and craft centres. It is set in a broad attractive valley that was much admired by Alexander von Humboldt (*see* panel, page 67).

### TOP ATTRACTIONS

\*\*\* **Mount Teide:** take the cable car up this volcano, Spain's highest mountain.
\*\*\* **Parque Nacional de las Cañadas del Teide:** the park around Mount Teide, full of amazing volcanic features.
\*\* **Museo de la Naturaleza y el Hombre:** Tenerife's top museum in Santa Cruz.
\*\* **Playa de las Teresitas:** Tenerife's best beach, composed of sand brought from the Sahara Desert.
\*\* **La Orotava Old Town:** stately streets and ancient houses with richly carved wooden balconies.

**Opposite:** *The summit of the Pico del Teide can be reached by cable car.*

With so much of interest in Tenerife for the visitor it is fortunate that the island has a good infrastructure of roads, allowing easy exploration. A motorway runs two thirds of the way around Tenerife, rental cars are cheap and coach excursions easily arranged. Whatever the interests of the visitor, Tenerife has all the ingredients for a wonderful holiday.

## THE LAND

Tenerife is one of the **Canary Islands**, an archipelago lying some 300km (186 miles) west of the African coast of Morocco. The islands belong to Spain, which is 1120km (696 miles) to the northeast. Tenerife lies on latitude 28° N, some 480km (300 miles) from the Tropic of Cancer. In addition to Tenerife, there are six other islands in the archipelago – Gran Canaria, Lanzarote, Fuerteventura, La Palma, La Gomera and El Hierro – plus some uninhabited islets. Together, the Canary Islands cover some 7500km² (2896 sq miles). They belong geographically to **Macronesia**, a group of islands (including Madeira and the Azores) of similar volcanic origins, topography and indigenous flora and fauna. The islands began to take form approximately 40 million years ago during the Tertiary geological era (about the same time as the Atlas Mountains in North Africa) as the African tectonic plate moved to the northeast,

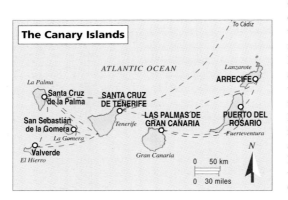

creating a weakness in the earth's crust out through which poured volcanic material. The Canary Islands can be thought of as the tips of undersea volcanoes. Looked at in this way, the peak of Mount Teide, in Tenerife, is around 7000m (23,000ft) above the sea floor. Fortunately, there is little volcanic activity in the Canary Islands today.

Volcanoes are regarded as extinct in Gran Canaria and Fuerteventura. The last eruptions took place on Lanzarote in 1824 and on Tenerife in 1909. The most recent was on La Palma in 1971.

**Above left:** *Mount Teide is snow-capped during the winter months.*

## Mountains and Rivers

Tenerife is dominated by **Mount Teide**, which at 3718m (12,198ft) is the highest mountain, not only in the Canary Islands, but also in the whole of Spain. It rises above the layers of clouds and seems to form the backdrop for views from all over the island. In clear conditions, Mount Teide can also often be seen from Gran Canaria and from the smaller islands to the west. In the winter months it has a capping of snow adding to its beauty, while in the summer the peak reveals layers of sulphurous ash. Around the peak is a huge depression called Las Cañadas, which is a caldera or collapsed crater. Nearby volcanic peaks include **Pico Viejo** (3105m/10,187ft) and **Montaña Blanca** (2750m/9022ft), while to the northwest is **Volcán Negro** (1626m/5334ft), the lava of which was responsible for devastating the northern port of Garachico in 1706. The most recent volcanic activity occurred in 1909, when **Mount Chinero**, to the northwest of Teide, poured out lava for 10 consecutive days. The volcanoes of the Teide complex are now dormant but geologists consider that further eruptions during the 21st century are a possibility.

**PLATE TECTONICS**

The theory of **Plate Tectonics** explains the distribution of the world's volcanoes. Derived from the **Theory of Continental Drift**, it shows that the earth's crust is divided into moveable plates. The plate boundaries are lines of weakness through which volcanic magma pours. This explains volcanoes in the mid-Atlantic where the American and European plates are moving apart. The Canary Islands are not on the mid-Atlantic ridge, but lie in an area of the crust's weakness caused by the movement that has built up the nearby Atlas Mountains in North Africa, as the African plate has drifted eastward.

*Above:* Puerto de la Cruz
*is a stylish resort on the*
*cloudier north of the island.*

A rocky volcanic ridge, known as the **Cumbre Dorsal**, leads to the northeast from Teide forming a backbone for most of the island. Occupying the tip of the peninsula, north of the capital Santa Cruz, are **Las Montañas de Anaga**. These basalt mountains are the result of one of the early lava flows and are, geologically speaking, the oldest part of Tenerife.

There are no permanent river courses in Tenerife, but there is evidence everywhere of erosion by rivers. Deep valleys run in a radial pattern from the highest points on the island, but running water is only found in them after winter rains or melting snow. These dry valleys, or *barrancos*, were probably formed during wetter periods of geological time.

A different type of landscape is found on the eastern side of Tenerife, where the low rainfall and lack of trees has created an area of arid **semi desert**, which has much in common with the Sahara, located some 300km (186 miles) to the east.

## Seas and Shores

Tenerife is surrounded by the deep waters of the **Atlantic Ocean**. Its erosive power shapes the coastline and over geological time the waves have worked on the volcanic rocks producing Tenerife's varied shoreline. The eastern coast is generally low-lying, but the remainder of the island has some spectacular cliffs, notably those in the west at **Los Gigantes**, which rise almost vertically to over 600m (nearly 2000ft). Tenerife's beaches are generally disappointing. Often they consist of unattractive black volcanic sand, although in places such as **Playa de las Teresitas**, near Santa Cruz, vast amounts of golden sand have been imported from the Sahara Desert. The lack of decent beaches is not, however, a handicap, as most apartments and hotels have excellent pools and in some other areas, such as **Puerto de la Cruz**, sea-water lido complexes have been built. Tenerife's Atlantic shoreline also ensures that almost every conceivable type of **water sport** can be catered for, including surfing, sail boarding, deep-sea fishing and scuba diving.

## Climate

The climate of Tenerife has been described as that of 'perpetual spring', although it can be more like continual summer in some of the island's more southerly resorts. There is, in fact, considerable climatic variety on the island depending on geographical position and the height of the land. The moist **trade winds** blow from a northeasterly direction, so that the windward northern coasts have more rain and cloud than the rest of the island. The leeward south and southwest of Tenerife are drier and hotter. These areas may have as much as 2500 hours of **sunshine** a year, and it is here that recent tourist development has concentrated. **Temperatures** vary from 18 to 24°C (65 to 75°F) in the summer and 16 to 20°C (61 to 68°F) in the winter, although afternoon temperatures during both seasons can be considerably higher. Occasionally in the summer the hot sirocco wind blows from the Sahara bringing desert dust, high temperatures and discomfort to all. **Rainfall** is generally light and varies from 750mm (29.5 in) on the north coast to 250mm (9.8 in) in the southwest. One interesting feature of the Tenerife climate is the layer of **cloud**, which, brought by the trade winds, lies on the windward side of the island between 500m (1650ft) and 1500m (4920ft). It may burn off during the afternoon, but can last for days, providing light rain for agriculture. The final climatic factor is the cool **Canary Current**. This flows from the north, ensuring that the sea temperatures around the island are lower than might be expected for this latitude: around 18°C (64.5°F) in the winter, and rising to 22°C (71°F) in the summer.

---

### TRADE WINDS AND CLOUDS

The persistent layer of cloud lying between 500m (1650ft) and 1500m (4920ft) is formed by the moist **trade winds** blowing off the Atlantic Ocean from a northeasterly direction. They are forced to rise by the mountains and then cool and condense forming clouds. These clouds bring the rain and moisture that provides the rich growing conditions for the luxuriant vegetation in the north of the island. Tourists should not worry too much about the clouds, which rarely cover the sunny resorts in the south of Tenerife. Nor should they be deterred from taking an excursion to the top of Mount Teide, as the cone of the volcano is usually in the sunshine several hundred feet above the cloud layer.

**Below:** *The Bird of Paradise flower or strelitzia is widely found in parks and hotel gardens.*

## Flora and Fauna

The varied altitude levels, the rich volcanic soil and the
amenable climate combine to make Tenerife a botanist's
paradise. There are a huge number of plants which are
indigenous to Tenerife. To this list can be added the
species of Mediterranean origin, brought in by the
Spaniards after the Conquest, plus exotic plants brought to
Tenerife by sailors and travellers from all over the world.

In the arid semi-desert areas in the south of the island,
drought resistant plants form scrubland. Especially
common are the euphorbias or **spurges**. Growing widely
are the candelabra spurge (which looks very much like a
cactus) and the various species of Canarian spurge. The
south of Tenerife also has large areas of crops cultivated
under plastic, including tomatoes and bananas, grown
with the aid of irrigation water. In the wetter north, the
lower levels are characterized by a wide variety of
tropical crops including oranges, dates and sugar cane.
The towns, cities and hotel gardens are bright with
introduced flowers and shrubs such as bougainvillea,
hibiscus, geraniums and strelitzia (or bird of paradise),
plus colourful trees such as jacaranda and mimosa.

At higher levels, where cloud is more frequent,
Canarian pines, eucalyptus and cork oak are common,
while poinsettias grow like weeds along the roadsides.
Under these conditions crops such as grapes, potatoes
and cereals thrive. In the **Anaga Mountains** in the
northeast of the island is one of the last remaining stands
of Canarian laurel, with associated heather, holly and

**Below:** *A viewpoint in the
Anaga Mountains gives a
fine vista along the northeastern coastline.*

linden. The highest part of
Tenerife is the area around
Mount Teide, known as
the **Cañadas National
Park**. This is the home of
the hardy Teide violet and
the remarkable Teide
viper's bugloss or *tajinaste*,
which every two years
produces a metre-long
spike of dramatic red

flowers. No account of Tenerife flora would be complete without a mention of the remarkable **Dragon tree** (*Dracaena draco*). Some specimens reach an impressive 18m (60ft) in height and can live for hundreds of years.

In contrast to the flora, the animal life of Tenerife is disappointing. Only 56 species of **birds** have been recorded as breeding in Tenerife; some have become extinct and many are only spasmodic breeders. Birdwatchers will be keen to see three species which are endemic to the Canary Islands – the blue chaffinch, the white-tailed laurel pigeon and the Bolles laurel pigeon. The last two are extremely rare. In addition, there are three Macronesian endemisms – the plain swift, Berthalots pipit and the wild canary – all of which are reasonably common. The only frequently seen raptors are kestrels, sparrowhawks and buzzards. Other common birds are Spanish sparrows, blackcaps, chiffchaffs, hoopoes and blackbirds. The visitor may also be surprised to see small flocks of noisy parrots that have escaped from theme parks and are able to survive well in the wild. All in all, Tenerife is not a noted ornithological site.

Amongst the **amphibians** and **reptiles** there are two frogs, three geckoes, a lizard and a skink. Geckoes are often found in houses, clinging to walls and ceilings where they deal effectively with insects and are regarded by the locals as signs of good luck. The large Canarian lizard, of which there are three subspecies in Tenerife, is abundant in stone walls, where it feeds on insects and plants.

With the exception of bats, all terrestial **mammals** in Tenerife were introduced by humans. There are six bats and all but one are common. Rabbits, house mice, hedgehogs and black and brown rats have been around for some time. The pygmy white-toothed shrew was first discovered in Tenerife in 1983 and has now spread over much of the island. It is the main source of food for buzzards and kestrels. Another recent introduction has

**Above:** *The large Canarian lizard is often seen in the crevices in stone walls.*

---

**THE CHRISTMAS WEED**

Growing along the verges of the rural roads of Tenerife are huge stands of **Poinsettia** (*Euphorbia pulcherrima*). This is surprising to the visitors from northern Europe, who normally associate the Poinsettia with potted plants at Christmas. In Tenerife, however, it grows almost like a weed. Originally from Mexico, it can reach heights of 2m (6.5ft). On top of the woody stems are small insignificant yellow flowers, surrounded by bright red leaves (which are often mistaken for the flowers).

**Above:** *Wild dolphins can be seen in the ocean around Tenerife. These captive specimens give displays at Loro Parque near Puerto de la Cruz.*

been the moufflon, which was released in the Cañadas National Park in 1971. However, research has shown that it is a serious threat to the indigenous flora and its numbers are now being controlled. **Marine mammals** are well represented and include a number of species of whale, porpoise and dolphin. Over 400 species of **fish** have been noted in the waters surrounding Tenerife. They include types of shark, tuna, stingrays and many of the fish that turn up on the menus in restaurants, such as hake, sardines and swordfish. Common shellfish include lobsters, prawns and mussels.

There is a wide range of **insects**, including the unwelcome mosquito. A few dragonflies are in evidence in the wetter areas, including the common scarlet darter. Among the endemic butterflies are the Canarian versions of the red admiral, grayling, speckled wood and cleopatra. Migrating monarchs can be abundant at certain times of the year.

## HISTORY IN BRIEF

The early history of the Canary Islands is shrouded in myth and mystery. The Greeks and the Romans certainly knew of their existence. Plato thought that they were the remains of the lost continent of Atlantis, while the geographer Ptolemy accurately located their position in AD150. It is highly unlikely, however, that either the Greeks or the Romans set foot on the Canary Islands. On the other hand, the Phoenicians and the Cathaginians almost certainly did.

### Early Inhabitants

Remains of **Cro Magnon Man** have been found on the Canary Islands. Examination of skulls showing people with broad faces and high foreheads, have been carbon-dated as ca. 3000BC. When European exploration of the

---

**THE DRAGON TREE**

Of all the trees in Tenerife, it is the **Dragon tree** *(Dracæna draco)* that is the most interesting and mysterious. The tree is believed to live for several centuries, but a precise dating is impossible as it does not produce tree rings. The tree has survived the Ice Age and is a remnant of the Tertiary era flora. Traditionally, Guanche meetings took place under a Dragon tree. They also used its sap (predictably called 'dragon's blood', as it turns bright red on exposure to air) to heal wounds, ward off evil spirits and to embalm their dead. The sap is also believed to be a cure for leprosy, and for a time it was exported to Italy to stain marble and violins.

## HISTORICAL CALENDAR

**3000BC–AD1500**
Archaeological evidence from skulls suggests the island was inhabited by Cro Magnon Man.
**1100BC** Phoenicians and Carthaginians are believed to have visited the Canary Islands.
**1312** Genoese explorer Lanzarotto Malocello occupies and names Lanzarote.
**1340** Portugal and Spain send ships to investigate the islands, finding Guanches living a Stone Age existence.
**1401** Spanish Conquest begins with Jean de Béthancourt taking Lanzarote, followed swiftly by La Gomera and Fuerteventura.
**1478** Juan Réjon attacks Gran Canaria, but takes a

further five years to subdue the Guanches.
**1483** Pedro de Viera is appointed the first Governor of the Canary Islands.
**1492** Columbus makes his first visit to the Canary Islands and observes Mount Teide erupting.
**1494** Tenerife is the last island to fall to the Spanish forces.
**16th and 17th centuries** The Spanish colonize the islands with the settlers developing a thriving economy, aided by the slave trade.
**1657** Admiral Blake destroys a Spanish treasure fleet near Santa Cruz.
**1797** Admiral Nelson's attempt to take Santa Cruz is repelled.

**1852** Isabella II declares the Canary Islands a free trade zone.
**Late 19th century** Bananas replace sugar cane as the mainstay of the Canary Islands' economy.
**1927** Canary Islands divided into two provinces, with Santa Cruz named the capital of the western province.
**1936** General Franco plots a military coup in Tenerife, which leads to the onset of the Spanish Civil War.
**1982** Regional constitution granted by Spain to the Canary Islands.
**1986** Canary Islands gain special status within the European Union.

islands took place in the 14th century, they found primitive people living there who were tall, blond and blue-eyed. They were known on Tenerife as **Guanches**, a name that is now applied to the early inhabitants of all the Canary Islands. Nobody is really certain of their origins (although most experts believe they were Berbers from North Africa) or how they got to the islands, as they appear to have had no knowledge of boat building.

## Guanche Society

Early European settlers found a primitive Stone Age society, with no knowledge of metals, the wheel, boat building or the bow and arrow. The majority lived in caves, although a few high-status Guanches had stone houses with straw roofs. Their economy was based on cattle rearing and the growing of crops. The women made pots that were highly decorated,

**Below:** *Ancient Guanche cave dwellings such as these can be found in many parts of the island.*

**FACTS AND FIGURES**

**Size:** 2057km² (794 sq miles)
**Population:** 665,000
**Capital:** Santa Cruz is the capital of both Tenerife and the western province of the Canary Islands
**Position:** 300km (186 miles) west of the African coast, 17°W and 27°N.
**Time Zone:** Follows GMT
**Language:** Spanish
**Religion:** Roman Catholic
**Highest Mountain:** Mount Teide at 3718m (12,198ft)
**Tourism:** Five million visitors per annum, providing 60 per cent of GNP.

using the coil method rather than the wheel. Clothing was made from sheep or goatskins. These animals also provided meat, cheese and milk. The Guanches also ate fish, fruit and *gofio*, which was roasted cereal flour.

Despite their primitive way of life, the Guanches had a sophisticated social structure. Tenerife was divided into nine kingdoms, each ruled by a *mencey* who was advised by a council of nobles known as a *tagoror*. The council usually met under an ancient Dragon tree, from where they administered justice. The Guanches were monogamous and women played a full part in society. There was no death penalty, but murderers were severely beaten and their possessions given to the relatives of their victims as compensation. The Guanches worshipped a god known as **Achaman**, who was closely linked with the sun, while Hell was believed to be in the Teide volcano. They also mummified their dead from the highest social strata, using skins and reeds, before laying them in special burial caves.

**Below:** *This reconstruction of a reed boat is on display at Güímar's Chacona Ethnographical Park.*

### The Spanish Conquest

The conquest of the Canary Islands by the Europeans began in 1312, when a Genoese explorer **Lanzarotto Malocello** conquered, and gave his name to, Lanzarote. Then followed years of squabbling between Spain and Portugal over the theoretical ownership of the islands, ending in 1401 with the islands being incorporated into the Spanish crown. European conquest began in earnest the following year when **Jean de Béthancourt** took Lanzarote for the King of Castile. By 1406 Béthancourt had also conquered Fuerteventura and La Gomera. Little further progress was made in the face of some determined Guanche resistance. Spain began a second phase of the Conquest in 1478, when Ferdinand and Isabella sanctioned an attack on Gran Canaria by **Juan Réjon**. He met fierce resistance and it was five years before the local Guanches were subdued. The next Spanish commander on the scene was **Alonso Fernández de Lugo**, who in 1491 received royal assent to attack La Palma and Tenerife. La Palma was quickly taken, but Tenerife was to prove the toughest island to overcome. De Lugo landed near the present day Santa Cruz in May 1493 with a force of 1000 soldiers plus 150 Guanche mercenaries from Gran Canaria. De Lugo negotiated with the nine *menceyes*, some of whom gave in peacefully. He then moved in on the remaining tribes, but his

forces were ambushed in the Barranco de Acentejo, suffering heavy losses. De Lugo went to Spain, recruited more men and returned to Tenerife later in the year. He had more success in a battle at La Laguna in November 1494, but the Guanche's resistance was far from over. Fortunately for de Lugo, a plague decimated Guanche numbers. The demoralized survivors were defeated at the second battle at Acentejo and the conquest was to all intents and purposes over.

**Above:** *Bronze statues of Guanche leaders line the promenade at Candelaria.*

## Post-Conquest Guanches

After the Conquest, Tenerife and its colonists were administered for Spain by *capitanes-generales*. Many Guanches died from diseases, introduced by the newcomers, to which they had no resistance. Large numbers of the Guanches were taken to Spain as slaves (although many were later allowed to return). Others interbred with the invaders, assumed Spanish names and were converted to Christianity. Assimilation with the colonists came swiftly and the Guanche's spoken language quickly disappeared. However, modern anthropological research claims that many of the Guanche characteristics remain in everyday life in the Canary Islands. Certainly a great number of the inhabitants of Tenerife are proud

### VERDINO DOGS

It is often claimed that the Canary Islands were named for the Latin *canus*, meaning 'dog'. Records mention large dogs found on the islands, and some researchers suggest that the inhabitants actually ate dogs. Certainly, the Conquistadors found that the Guanches kept dogs to guard their flocks. The invaders feared the dogs and passed a law allowing each shepherd only one dog. Known as *verdinos* for their greenish tinge, the dogs were smooth-haired with broad jaws. Today, as part of the revived nationalism of the Canarios, there is a movement to keep the Verdino strain pure and have it confirmed as a registered breed.

**Above:** *Vineyards in the north of the island; the peak period of wine production was in the 18th century.*

of their Guanche ancestry, as they like to feel that this highlights the differences between themselves and the mainland Spaniards.

## Spanish Colonial Rule

For the next three centuries, the Canary Islands experienced mixed fortunes under Spanish colonial rule. The islands attracted large number of settlers, not only from Spain, but also from Portugal, France and Italy. After Columbus's discovery of the New World in 1492, the Canary Islands became an important staging post for ships travelling to and from the Americas. Any territory owned by Spain, however, was fair game for corsairs and the Barbary pirates who frequently raided the islands. The fleets of Britain, France, Holland and Portugal made numerous attempts to take the Canaries, without lasting success. There were some spectacular British naval engagements off Tenerife. In 1657, Blake totally destroyed a Spanish treasure fleet near Santa Cruz. Nelson was less fortunate in 1797 when he not only failed to subdue Santa Cruz, but lost his right arm in the battle as well.

## Boom and Bust

During the years of colonial rule, the Canary Islands in general and Tenerife in particular, experienced varied economic fortunes. Reliance on various types of monoculture led to cycles of 'boom and bust', with the downturns leading to mass emigration to the New World. In the early 16th century, **sugar cane** was introduced from Asia. The industry was able to use slave labour and sugar became Tenerife's main source of income. The abolition of slavery in 1537 and the cheaper sugar produced in Brazil and Central America, led to the collapse of the industry. The cultivation of sugar cane was replaced by the production of **wine**, particularly on Tenerife. The vines produced a strong sherry-like wine known as 'malmsey' or what Shakespeare referred to as Canary Sack. It was very popular in Elizabethan England

---

### CHRISTOPHER COLUMBUS

Christopher Columbus had many connections with the Canary Islands. When he was making his four transatlantic crossings, the Canary Islands were the last landfall before setting sail to cross the ocean, and provided the opportunity to take on provisions and wait for favourable winds. For Columbus there were also other reasons for a visit. Living on La Gomera, was Beatriz de Bobadilla, a former mistress of King Ferdinand of Spain. Columbus had a 'romance' with Beatriz and certainly stopped at La Gomera on his first three transatlantic voyages. By the time of his fourth voyage, Beatriz had married Alonso de Lugo, one of the most powerful men in the islands – on this occasion Columbus wisely gave La Gomera a miss!

and at the height of its production some 10,000 barrels were sent to London annually. Many of the fine buildings in the historic towns of Tenerife were constructed on the profits of the wine trade. Unfortunately the success of the wine trade was not to last. Changing tastes, disease of the vines and the success of the rival Madeira wine, meant that by the start of the 19th century the wine boom was over. This led inevitably to further emigration, mainly to Venezuela and Cuba.

In 1825, a new product came on the scene. This was **cochineal**, a red dye that was extracted from a small insect which was parasitic on cactus plants. Thousands of prickly pear cactus plants soon appeared in many parts of Tenerife as this unusual type of farming boomed. By the 1870s, however, chemical dyes began to appear on the market and the cochineal trade fell away. More emigration!

Meanwhile, there were important political developments. The Canary Islands were declared a province of Spain in 1821, with Santa Cruz de Tenerife named the capital. Inter-island rivalry was never far from the surface and in 1912 Spain introduced Island Councils or *Cabildos*. In 1927 the Spanish Government divided the Canary Islands into two provinces – an eastern province comprising Lanzarote, Fuerteventura and Gran Canaria, with its capital at Las Palmas, and a western province made up of Tenerife and the smaller islands of La Gomera, El Hierro and La Palma, with the capital at Santa Cruz de Tenerife.

The economy of the Canary Islands showed an upturn during the late 19th and early 20th centuries, helped by their designation as a free trade zone and the growth of the Atlantic steamship trade. In the 1850s, British entrepreneurs introduced banana production to the islands, and by the turn of the century there were banana

### BATTLE OF NELSON'S ARM

It is probably true to say that few of the thousands of English tourists who visit the Canary Islands annually, realize that their national hero, Admiral Horatio Nelson, lost a battle (and his arm) in a naval engagement at Tenerife. After the Spanish Conquest and the discovery of the Americas, the Canary Islands enjoyed a period of prosperity. This made ports, such as Santa Cruz de Tenerife, a popular target for both pirates and the ships of rival seafaring nations. In 1797, Nelson was instructed to seize the port. His assault, however, was a failure, due to rough seas and the staunch defence of the townspeople. During the battle, Nelson lost his right arm to cannon fire. His flotilla escaped, and this was Nelson's only defeat in an illustrious career.

**Below:** *Lush banana plantations are found in the wetter parts of the north of the island.*

## THE BUTCHER BIRD

One interesting bird among the rather small avian population of Tenerife is the Great Grey Shrike (*Lanius excubitor*). The size of a blackbird, this handsome black, grey and white bird spends much of its time on a perch or telephone wire waving its tail and watching for prey. It can often be seen in the Teide National Park, where it catches small birds, mice, lizards and insects. Its habit of impaling its prey on thorns or barbed wire 'larders' has led to its title of the 'butcher bird'.

**Below:** *Memorial to those who fell in the Spanish Civil War. The monument is located in the Plaza de España in Santa Cruz.*

plantations across many of the wetter parts of Tenerife. Although bananas are still produced in Tenerife today, the disruption caused by two world wars and the competition from Central and South America led to a slump in production. The result was a further wave of emigration to the Americas. The extent of this emigration is illustrated by the fact that over a quarter of a million people of Canary Island origin are estimated to live in Caracas, the capital of Venezuela.

## The Rise of Franco

During the 1930s Tenerife found itself involved in the Spanish Civil War. In March 1936, General Franco – who was suspected of planning a coup to overthrow the government – was 'exiled' to Tenerife with the post of *Commandante-General*. Franco was on Tenerife for a mere four months, but during this time he survived no fewer than three assassination attempts while he planned his next coup. The action began in Morocco, and Franco quickly flew there to lead the insurgents. Thus began the brutal Civil War that was to divide towns and families. Two days after Franco's departure, the fascists took control of Tenerife.

## The Growth of Tourism

Despite Spain's historic links with Tenerife, the Canary Islands were largely neglected during Franco's years in power, giving rise to an active separatist movement in the archipelago. The movement was only stemmed in 1982, when the Canaries (and other parts of Spain) were given autonomous powers and a regional constitution. Another factor that quelled nationalism was the growth of **tourism**, which is now Tenerife's main source of convertible revenue.

**Above:** *The colours of the Canary Islands' flag were taken from the naval flags of Santa Cruz de Tenerife and Las Palmas.*

# GOVERNMENT AND ECONOMY
## Government

The two provinces of the Canary Islands form one of the 17 autonomous regional communities in Spain. Rivalry between the islands is traditional and the regional government has offices in both Santa Cruz de Tenerife and Las Palmas on Gran Canaria. The regional government has powers covering transport, agriculture, health and policing, and can raise local taxes. Each island has a local administration (the *cabildo*), while a further level of administration known as the district or *municipio* is also in place.

The main **political parties** are the left wing Partido Socialista Obrero Español (PSOE) and the right of centre Partido Popular (PP). In the 1990s the various nationalist groups merged to form the Coalición Canaria (CC) which, rather than pressing for independence, now works for a better deal from Madrid. In the 1999 elections CC was the largest party, but in 2004 it lost two-thirds of its seats to the main parties. Most recent governments have been coalitions between the various parties.

## The Economy

Canarian **agriculture** has learnt that monoculture does not pay in the long run, and most farms have a variety of enterprises. Crops here include bananas, tomatoes, tobacco, coffee, citrus fruit and exotic fruits and flowers.

**BERTHALOT'S PIPIT**

This unassuming little brown bird is endemic to the Canary Islands and found in dry places from sea level to the higher parts of Mount Teide. It is often seen on the ground in small family groups seeking insects, and will allow people to approach quite closely before flying off. But how did it get its strange title? It was, in fact, named by Sabin Berthalot, the French Consul in Santa Cruz, who introduced bananas and cochineal to the island in the 19th century. He also collaborated with the British naturalist FB Webb to write the Natural History of the Canary Islands.

Animal husbandry is quite rare and confined to a few goats, sheep and cattle. Agricultural production is helped by the fertile volcanic soil, the equable climate and the use of plastic greenhouses and irrigation. Water supply is a constant problem these days, as precipitation totals have dropped and the demands of tourism have increased. Much use is made of volcanic clinker to conserve soil moisture levels.

The **Manufacturing industry** accounts for only 9 per cent of the island's GDP. Tax discounts are designed to attract business to the island and IVA (the Spanish equivalent of VAT) is only 4.5 per cent, compared with 16 per cent on the mainland. The **tertiary sector** of industry is dominated by **tourism**. The Canary Islands are an all-year-round destination attracting over 8 million visitors annually, mainly from Britain, Germany, Scandinavia, Holland and mainland Spain. This income has had the effect of improving the island's infrastructure to the benefit of *Canarios* and visitors alike. Nevertheless, unemployment figures are high at 16 per cent and average wages are among the lowest in the EU. The economy of the Canary Islands is currently boosted by several billion Euros annually due to its status as one of the EU's Ultra-Peripheral Regions (UPRs).

## THE PEOPLE

The total **population** of the Canary Islands currently stands at 1,620,000 and grows at more than 1 per cent annually. At the last census, Tenerife had 665, 562 inhabitants, including a good number of foreign residents, mainly from Britain and Germany. There are also small numbers from the Americas, mainly returning emigrants from countries such as Cuba and Venezuela. The people from Tenerife are known locally as *Tinerfeños*. They are mainly descended from Spaniards and are generally dark haired with an olive complexion. They are fiercely patriotic, regarding

---

**WOODEN BALCONIES**

There is a long tradition of wood carving in Tenerife that is shown to good advantage in the Plateresque style used widely in churches during the 16th and 17th centuries. With plenty of Canarian pine available, it was inevitable that the style would spread into domestic architecture. The pine is easily carved but also very durable and best seen in the intricately carved balconies of the fine mansions of the country, particularly in the older parts of La Laguna and La Orotava.

themselves as *Canarios*, rather than from the *peninsular* as they call mainland Spain. They have mixed feelings towards mainland Spaniards, calling them *godos* (or Goths) and accusing them of taking local jobs. Indeed many *Canarios* like to think of themselves as African rather than Spanish.

Like the mainland Spanish, *Canarios* are family-orientated. Machismo is still a feature of male life, but women have become increasingly liberated and now take a full part in public life, with many being employed in the tourist industry.

## Language

The official language on Tenerife is **Castilian Spanish**, but pronunciation is more akin to Spanish spoken in Andalucía or South America. The lisping 'th' applied to 'c' and 'z' is replaced by an 's' sound. Consonants at the ends of words are often omitted, so that *gracias* becomes *gracia*. Some words borrowed from South American Spanish are in common use, such as the Cuban *gua gua* (pronounced *wah wah*) for autobus. *Tinerfeños* always appreciate an attempt to speak their language, so bring a good phrase book and dictionary.

Some **Guanche** words have survived, mainly in place names. **English** is widely spoken in the tourist industry.

### EMIGRATION

Throughout the history of the Canary Islands emigration has been a continuing theme, usually coinciding with down-turns in the economy. Ships crossing the Atlantic frequently stopped to refuel in the Canary Islands and it was easy to book a passage. The usual destination was Latin America, where Spanish was universally spoken. A favourite destination in the early years was Cuba where emigrants from the Canaries played an important role in the growth of the capital, Havana, and in the development of the cigar-making industry. During the difficult days of the Spanish Civil War, and later World War II, there was renewed emigration, this time to Venezuela. However, with the growth of tourism there has been plenty of work and little need to emigrate. In fact, many northern Europeans are immigrants to the Canary Islands.

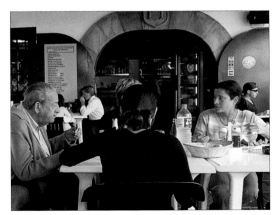

**Opposite:** *A wide variety of fruit is produced on Tenerife, but many agricultural workers have left the land to work in the tourist industry.*
**Left:** *Tinerfeños enjoy their weekends, when eating out is a popular pastime.*

**Below:** *A church front on
La Gomera island; village
churches are well cared for.*

## Religion

The Spanish conquerors brought **Roman Catholicism**
with them to the Canary Islands and they swiftly
converted the Guanches. It is still the official religion
and it plays an important part in people's lives.
Although weekly church attendance is not high,
most *Tinerfeños* have church baptisms, weddings and
funerals and support religious feast days. There are a
number of churches of other denominations, plus two
synagogues and a mosque.

## Festivals

Fiestas are the traditional way of celebrating saints' days
on the religious calendar. These include *Candelaria*, the
patron saint of the Canary Islands; *Corpus Christi*, when
floral carpets are laid out on the streets; Easter, which
usually involves statues of the Virgin being paraded
through the streets; and *Nuestra Señora de la Luz* marked
by processions of boats. **Romerias** are processions led by
decorated ox carts which head from town churches to a
hermitage or similar location. Other festivals are of a
secular nature and may include week-long *ferias* or

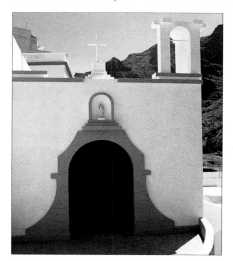

fairs. Outstanding is the **Carnaval**
(Carnival) at Santa Cruz, which
rivals that at Rio. Fiestas are usually
accompanied by fireworks, bonfires,
parades, traditional singing and folk
dancing. Some festivals, such as the
Rain Festival at Telde, are believed to
date back to the times of the
Guanches, while on other occasions
old historical events are acted out.

## Sport and Recreation

The Canary Islands have some
unique forms of sport that go back
centuries and are enthusiastically
followed by the locals. **Lucha
Canaria**, or Canarian Wrestling,
probably had its origin in Guanche

trials of strength. Bull fighting is not popular in the Canary Islands, but sand covered arenas resembling bullrings are used for the wrestling competitions. The rules are strict. There are two teams of 12 participants or *luchadores*. Two contestants at a time attempt to throw each other to the ground in a best of three competition or *brega*. Only the soles of the feet must touch the ground. Canarian wrestling is not a violent sport, as punching and kicking are not allowed. Skill and balance are more important than weight and size. The team which wins the most *bregas* claims the overall match. *Luchas* are often held at original Guanche locations and at fiestas. **Juego del Palo**, or stick fighting, also originated in pre-Conquest days. It is a contest using 2m (6.5ft) wooden staves called *banot*. Even longer staves of around 2.5m (8ft) are used in the **salto del regaton de la garrocha**, a form of pole vaulting in which contestants leap down the mountainside and across deep ravines. Less appealing to tourists will be **cock fighting**, which has a strong following in Tenerife.

The more international spectator sports are also hugely popular in the Canary Islands. As in the rest of Spain, **football** is obsessively followed. Club Deportivo Tenerife are in the Spanish Second Division and their local derbys against rivals UD Las Palmas are among the highlights of the sporting year. Other sports include beach volleyball, tennis and golf. There are many possibilities for **water sports**, both for locals and tourists. **Sailing**, **water skiing**, **windsurfing** and **power-boat racing** are all highly popular. The clear, warm Atlantic is ideal for **scuba diving** and **snorkelling** and there are a number of underwater national parks around the island. The ocean also provides ideal conditions for **deep-sea fishing**. Charter boats are available to catch marlin, tunny, shark and swordfish.

**Above:** *El Médano, with its persistent winds, is the best windsurfing spot on the island.*

### WALKERS AND DOGS

Tenerife has some superb walking country, particularly in the Anaga Mountains, the Teno Massif and in the Mount Teide National Park. A common problem in the first two areas is the attention that walkers receive from dogs. In most cases their bark is worse than their bite, and even the more ferocious will be deterred by a walking stick or the action of picking up a stone. For particularly nervous hikers there are ultrasonic dog-scarers that can be used. A different sort of problem is the over-friendly dog who latches on to you and just will not go away!

**Above:** *Traditional pottery-making has changed little since Guanche times.*
**Opposite:** *A statue of poet and novelist Ángel Guimerá.*

---

### GUANCHE ARTISTIC SEALS

Although the Guanches had no knowledge of metals, the wheel or the bow and arrow, they were certainly not without artistic ability, particularly with regard to ceramics. They made pots with the coil method rather than using a wheel, and produced a wide range of other ceramic goods, including jewellery and small symbolic figurines (replicas of which can be bought in shops). The **Museo de la Naturaleza y el Hombre** in Santa Cruz has hundreds of examples of small ceramic discs that have been painted or etched with designs, usually of a geometric kind. They tend to be described as 'artistic seals', but their true purpose is debatable. Were they for personal ornamentation, a form of currency or for pressing into clay to conclude business? We may never know.

---

## Crafts

Tourists find that there is a wide variety of craft articles available to take home as souvenirs. Indeed, for many of the inhabitants in the rural villages of the island, the production of craft items is a major source of income. Sadly, however, many of the items on sale in souvenir shops are cheap imitations from abroad and this is a major threat to the survival of ancient craft skills.

Many of the handicrafts that are so admired by tourists, were in fact essential to the daily agricultural way of life in past centuries. The **woodworking** skills can be seen on the ornately carved balconies of the older towns of Tenerife and on furniture and cedarwood chests. The main wood-carving centres are at La Laguna and La Orotava. **Basketwork**, using wood, cane, straw and palm leaves, is a common craft throughout the island. Examples include straw hats, fans, baskets and bags. The craft of **pottery** dates right back to Guanche times and it is still made in the traditional way without using a wheel. The pots vary in size from the large urns which were once used to store olive oil, down to small vases and ashtrays. Look out for the small Guanche-style figurines. Probably the most attractive souvenirs (and the lightest to carry home) are the **textiles**. Embroidered cloth is seen to advantage in the colourful national costumes that are worn at local festivals. Tablecloths, napkins and handkerchiefs are the most commonly displayed items, but these are also the craft goods that are brought in from abroad. Look for the genuine articles at the schools of embroidery, such as that at the Casa de los Balcones at La Orotava. Other interesting craft souvenirs are the rag dolls in national costume, musical instruments such as the local *timple*, items made from polished volcanic stone and lacework made by the island's nuns.

## The Arts

Although the Guanches left numerous examples of wall paintings in caves, it was some time before any notable Spanish **painters** emerged. Most of the 17th-, 18th- and 19th-century artists confined their work to religious topics and some of their paintings may be seen in the churches of the island. During the 20th century, the island's main Impressionist artist was Manuel González Méndez (1843–1909). Another well-known artist was Néstor de la Torre (1887–1938), who specialized in murals and was responsible for a campaign to revive Canarian folk art and architecture. The work of the versatile César Manrique, artist, architect and environmentalist, can be seen throughout the Canary Islands, particularly in the design of outdoor swimming complexes.

As far as **sculpture** is concerned, the name of José Luján Pérez (1756–1815) stands out. His work can be found in churches and cathedrals throughout the Canary Islands. Although the Guanches had no written language, **literature** has a long history in the Canary Islands. Indeed there is a well-known saying 'the Canaries is a land of poets'. Certainly there have been many novelists and poets over the centuries, but most of them have had to move to the mainland to gain recognition. Some of the best-known are José de Viera y Clavijo (1731–1813), Benito Pérez Galdós (1843–1920) and Angel Guimerá (1849–1924).

There are some fine museums and art galleries in the Canary Islands. On Tenerife, try to visit the Museo de la Naturaleza y el Hombre and the Museo Municipal de Bellas Artes in Santa Cruz. The former, located in the old city hospital, has a superb display of Guanche culture. In La Orotava, the Casa Tafuriaste has an outstanding collection of ceramics. The Casa de Carta ethnological museum displays a comprehensive collection of regional costumes.

---

**GUANCHE SKULL PIERCING**

In the Museo de la Naturaleza y El Hombre in Santa Cruz are around 1000 skulls dating back to Guanche times. Many of them show the drilled holes that were typical of the Guanches. In the medical world, the process is known as 'trepanning' and is carried out with metal drills. However, the Guanches had no knowledge of metals, so they must have carried out this custom with stone – probably the volcanic rock known as obsidian. Why did they carry out this gruesome practice? Was it to let evil spirits out? Was it done while they were living or after they died? The questions remain unanswered.

## THE UNUSUAL *TIMPLE*

On the island of Tenerife, most traditional dancing and songs are accompanied by the *timple* (pronounced 'tim-play'). It is a wooden, stringed instrument closely akin to the ukelele and the mandolin. It is made of wood and has a rounded back. It normally has five strings, although there is a four-string version called the *contra*, which is found on Lanzarote. Once thought to have originated from the Spanish *guitarillo*, it is now believed to have been brought to the islands by Berber slaves. Whenever there is a local fiesta, the *timple* will be much in evidence. It was even exported to Latin American countries with the many waves of emigrants and it figures strongly in the folk music of Cuba and Venezuela. The souvenir shops at Tenerife airport sell CDs featuring *timple* music and they make a fitting momento of a holiday on the island.

## Music and Dance

Although the Canary Islands have not produced any noted composers, classical music is taken seriously and the Tenerife Symphony Orchestra is well supported. The orchestra is now based at the Auditorio de Tenerife – a spectacular new concert hall in Santa Cruz. Traditional folk music and dancing are always prominent in fiesta times. Dances include the lively *isa* and the more dignified *folia*. Occasionally the *tajaraste* may be performed. This dance is believed to have had its origins in Guanche times. The dancing is accompanied by traditional instruments such as castanets (*characas*) and the *timple* (*see* panel, this page). Many dances, such as the *malagueña* and the *sevillaña*, have been introduced by immigrants from Andalucía. Popular music, on the other hand, seems to have been influenced from the other direction, with dominant Latin American *salsa* rhythms.

## Architecture

The Guanches, who were largely cave dwellers, left little legacy in the way of vernacular architecture. The oldest buildings in Tenerife, therefore, date back to the Spanish Conquest. Since this time, no destructive wars have occurred and this fact, combined with the mild weather, has meant that many of the island's ancient buildings are in a good state of preservation.

The Gothic style was going out of fashion at the time of the Conquest, with the result that many of the early buildings were constructed in the **Mudéjar** style, which had been bequeathed to the Spaniards by the Moors. In domestic design, the *Mudéjar* style encompasses the need for water and protection from the sun. Most houses are built around a central courtyard or *patio*, frequently with a decorated well. In the larger houses, the *patio* had shady trees and a colonnaded cloister. This scheme was also common on the front of the house, with a columned, covered walkway at ground level and a balcony at first floor level. The balconies were made of wood and often highly decorated. There are some superb examples of this colonial style in the old parts of La Laguna and La Orotava.

**Opposite:** *A typical Canarian balcony like this one can be found in many of the older towns.*

Artisans' houses from the same period are much simpler stone and whitewashed buildings, which feature predominantly flat roofs in the drier south of the island and tiled roofs in the wetter parts.

There is a good way of dating houses in Tenerife – up to the end of the 17th century windows were often placed irregularly, but from the 17th century onwards house frontages became symmetrical, with a central door and equal-sized windows. A number of other architectural styles can be seen in Tenerife. By the 16th century, the *Mudéjar* style had been replaced with the intricate ***Plateresque***, named after the work of silversmiths and particularly evident in some of the carved ceilings. By the 19th century, **Portuguese Baroque** had appeared, typified by the ornate iron railings on balconies. During the same period, public buildings such as town halls and museums were being constructed in the **neoclassical** style. The early 20th century saw some interesting **Art Nouveau** buildings, mainly the work of César Manrique. The second half of the century saw the growth of tourism and with it some rather ugly multistorey apartment blocks. More recent tourist development is of the low-rise variety and much more sympathetic to the environment.

## TENERIFE'S CHURCHES

Tenerife has only one cathedral, but it does have several marvellous churches. Many date from the early 16th century and display a variety of styles. Few are genuinely Gothic, but there are many in the *Mudéjar* style, from the Moorish occupation of southern Spain. Others display the ornate plateresque decoration. Some have carved wooden ceilings. Stained-glass windows are generally uninspiring, but this is more than compensated for by superb interiors. Altar screens (*retablos*) are often highly carved and dripping with gold leaf. Many churches have wooden carvings by Luján Pérez (1756–1815), the greatest of the Canarian sculptors. Remember that beachwear is inappropriate in churches and not appreciated by the locals.

## Food and Drink

The **food** of Tenerife illustrates a wide range of influences from other countries, including mainland Spain, northern Europe and even the Americas. Typically Canarian food is most likely to be found in the capital, Santa Cruz, and in the more rural areas, rather than in the main resorts where restaurants tend to serve food of an international persuasion. The visitor must first adjust to the unusual meal times in Tenerife (outside the hotels). **Breakfast** (*desayuno*) is generally light and rarely provided before 09:30. It usually consists of coffee, a sandwich (*bocadillo*) or a small cake (*pastel*). **Lunch** (*almuerzo*) is taken late, rarely before 14:30 and may have been preceded by **tapas**, which are light snacks served at the bar. Lunch for many *Tinerfeños* will be the main meal of the day. **Dinner** (*cena*) is a lighter meal for the locals, who would rarely think of eating before 22:00.

There are two items of Canarian food which should be sampled. The traditional island staple food, going back to Guanche times is *gofio*, which is ground and toasted wheat or maize. Served with most main courses are *papas arugadas*, which are small new potatoes with wrinkly skins which have been boiled in very salty water.

**Main meals** usually begin with a 'starter' such as salad (*ensalada*) or soup (*sopa*). Particular favourites are fish soup (*sopa de pescado*) and vegetable soup (*sopa de verdura*). Most restaurants will also offer the mainland cold soup *gazpacho*, which consists of tomatoes, onions and garlic. The main course will usually involve meat (*carne*) or fish (*pescado*). The most commonly offered meats are beef (*ternera*), chicken (*pollo*), lamb (*cordero*), pork (*cerdo*) and rabbit (*conejo*). The prolific wild rabbits are shot widely on the islands, but others are reared domestically for the table. The meat may be grilled (*a la parilla*), roasted (*asado*) or come in a stew (*estofado* or *puchero*). A mouth watering variety of **fish** and **shellfish** can be found on the menu. Fish is usually prepared simply, being fried or grilled (*a la plancha*). At some of the better fish restaurants, it is possible to choose your own fish from a tank or a cold cabinet. You then pay by weight. The most common fish on the menu are sea bass (*cherne*), hake (*merluza*), swordfish (*pez espada*), sole (*lenguado*), tuna (*atún* or *bonito*) and parrot fish (*vieja*). Some excellent shellfish can be found, including prawns (*gambas*), mussels (*mejillones*) and squid (*calamares*). Particular Tenerife specialities are the sauces which are provided with both fish and meat dishes. The red *mojo rojo* is a spicy vinaigrette-type sauce made from a mixture of chilli, cumin, paprika and saffron, usually served with meat. *Mojo verde* is a green variation with coriander or parsley used instead of paprika, making a perfect accompaniment to fish. Vegetables are rather limited on the Tenerife menu and salad is usually served as a garnishing with most main dishes.

The choice of **desserts** (*postres*) is usually confined to traditional Spanish favourites such as crème caramel (*flan*), ice cream (*helado*) or fruit (*fruta*). Any local **cheese**

---

**NIBBLES – SPANISH STYLE**

*Tapas* are believed to have originated in Seville during the 19th century, when drinkers protected their glass of *fino* from dust, flies and dripping hams by putting a cover or *tapa* over their glass. The cover was often a slice of bread, on which enterprising bartenders began to add food. The rest, as they say, is history. Spain's quirky mealtimes encourage 'grazing' – taking the occasional snack to fill the gap. The days when a free *tapa* was provided with a drink are over, but a *tapas crawl* is one of the delights of Tenerife, particularly in the capital, Santa Cruz. *Tapas* vary from a simple dish of olives or a slice of cheese, to quite sophisticated dishes. Remember that it is cheaper to take your *tapas* standing at a bar, than sitting at a table.

**Opposite:** Papas aru-gadas, *strongly salted new potatoes, accompany most main course dishes.*
**Left:** *Squid* – calamares *or* pulpa – *can be prepared in a variety of ways.*

## TENERIFE'S WINES

The Canary Islands have a long history of wine-making starting with Canary Sack, or Malmsey, which was well-known to Shakespeare. The demand for such fortified wines has declined and today more traditional wines are produced. Some 10 per cent of the agricultural land is given over to vines, the production helped by the climate and rich volcanic soil. In recent years there has been an emphasis on quality control, which means that little of the table wine finds its way onto the supermarket shelves. Instead, it is bought by the locals directly from the vineyards. Fortunately for tourists, there is plenty of decent wine brought in from mainland Spain.

on offer will be unusual, such as the Tenerife white goat's cheese (*queso blanco*). Another interesting speciality is *queso de flor*, which is a mixture of cow's and sheep's milk flavoured with the flowers of a thistle.

The main resort areas of Tenerife also offer a bewildering selection of foreign restaurants. Chinese and Indian restaurants are particularly common, but many other nationalities are represented. Visitors on a budget should try the menu of the day (*menu del dia*), which usually offers a starter, a main course and a sweet, plus a drink, for a bargain price.

Sampling **alcoholic drinks** is an essential part of many people's holiday and Tenerife offers plenty of choice, including some local specialities. The production of **wine** has a long history on the island, providing a considerable amount of Malmsey or Canary Sack to Elizabethan England. Made from the sweet Malvesia grape, there is still a small amount of Malmsey in production today, but Tenerife cannot compete with Madeira for this type of wine. The quality of Tenerife's table wines has improved greatly in recent years, with red wines produced in the areas around Tacorante, Santa Ursula and La Victoria. White and rosé wines come from

Icod de los Vinos and La Guancha, and some have gained *denominación de origen* status. Most of the Tenerife wines are produced for local consumption, so to satisfy the demands of hotels and restaurants, a large amount of wine is imported from mainland Spain. There are some popular wine-based summer drinks including *tinto de verano*, a mixture of red wine and lemonade, and the deceptively strong *sangria*, which is a combination of red wine, liqueurs and lemonade garnished with ice and fruit. The local **beer** in Tenerife is the very drinkable *Dorada*, which is sold in bottled and draught form. For a small draught beer ask for *una caña*. A full range of foreign beers is also available. Amongst the **spirits** are some popular mainland brandies (*coñac*) such as *Sobrerano* and *Fundador*. The best known local spirit is rum (*ron*), which is made from sugar cane. Another variety is *ron miel*, a rum liqueur with added honey. There are a number of other **liqueurs**, many of which are made from the sub tropical fruits grown on Tenerife. The most popular is *cobana*, a yellow banana liqueur that comes in a striking bottle. Remember that measures of spirits are two or three times more than one would expect at home!

**Above:** *The popular Dorada beer, which is produced in Tenerife.*
**Opposite:** *Local wines rarely reach hotels and supermarkets, which prefer varieties from the mainland.*

The most popular of the **non-alcoholic drinks** is coffee, which comes in a variety of forms. Any bar with a reputation will make their coffee in an 'espresso' machine and for an espresso-type coffee ask for either a *café solo* (which is black) or a *café cortado* (which has just a touch of milk). *Café con leche* is a milky coffee. Don't be surprised to find that your coffee arrives in a glass. *Canarios* often take a shot of rum in their coffee or have an accompanying *coñac*. Tea is also available, but is usually served rather weak. Chocolate is a popular breakfast drink for *Tinerfeños* and is usually consumed with *churros* (a form of doughnut). There is a full range of soft drinks (*refrescos*) and fruit juices (*zumos*).

---

**UFO's**

Is it the clear air of Tenerife or is it the strength of the local wines? Whatever the answer, the fact remains that this island has one of the highest percentages of claims to have seen **unidentified flying objects**. The north of Tenerife, particularly in the Punta de Hidalgo area, has most of the sightings.

# 2
# Santa Cruz de Tenerife

Santa Cruz de Tenerife – more widely known as just Santa Cruz – is the capital of both Tenerife and the western province of the Canary Islands, which includes the islands of La Gomera, La Palma and El Hierro. It is a bustling modern city with over 200,000 inhabitants (one third of the island's inhabitants), covering an area of 150km² (58 sq miles). The suburbs spread north to the Anaga Mountains and southwest towards the Cumbre Dorsal. Santa Cruz shares the government of the Canary Islands with Las Palmas (on Gran Canaria). It is one of the largest ports in Spain, benefiting historically from transatlantic trade. The port has adapted to modern times and today the emphasis is on containers and cruise liners.

The city has a long history, going back to the arrival of the **Conquistadors** in 1494. Although many of Santa Cruz's historic buildings have been lost to modern development, sufficient remain to create a pleasant atmosphere in the central area of the city. However, only a small minority of the tourists who come to Tenerife visit Santa Cruz. This is a pity as the city makes an interesting day trip, with its sea front promenade, leafy squares, historic churches and excellent museums. Some tour operators run coach trips to Santa Cruz for the express purpose of shopping. Since Santa Cruz became a 'free port' in 1852 it has been able to sell its goods duty free, offering many shopping bargains. For the independent traveller there is much more to see than shops. From the central square, the Plaza de España, the sights of interest are within easy walking distance.

## DON'T MISS

**\*\*\* Museo de la Naturaleza y el Hombre:** information on the way of life of the ancient Guanches.
**\*\* Iglesia de Nuestra Señora de la Concepción:** a church with an octagonal tower and a lovely interior.
**\* Mercado de Nuestra Señora de Africa:** Santa Cruz's busy market.
**\* Parque Municipal García Sanabria:** a shady park and gardens – a peaceful break from the bustle of the city.
**\* Parque Marítimo:** César Manrique's beautifully designed sea water lido built on derelict dockland.

**Opposite:** *View over Santa Cruz and the harbour.*

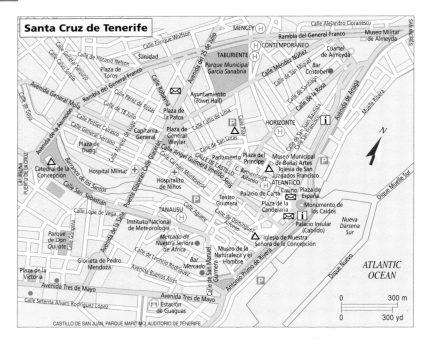

## THE HISTORY OF SANTA CRUZ

Santa Cruz's history really began on 3 May 1494, when **Alonso Fernández de Lugo** landed on the beach which the Guanches called Añaza. De Lugo planted his Holy Cross on the beach and it was from this cross that the city acquired its name. A fortress was quickly built to defend the settlement and de Lugo set about subduing the Guanches, a task which was to take many years. Santa Cruz was slow to grow. La Laguna was the first capital of the island and Garachico, on the north of the island and facing the New World, became the chief port. However, Garachico was largely destroyed by a volcanic eruption in 1706 and business moved to Santa Cruz. By the 18th and 19th centuries, aided by the slave trade and transatlantic commerce, the port of Santa Cruz was flourishing, and in 1723 it replaced La Laguna as the island's capital.

---

### CLIMATE

Santa Cruz is in the cloudier and wetter north of the island, but its coastal position in the rain shadow of the Anaga Mountains, means that it often escapes the cloud and rain that is found inland at higher altitude. **Rainfall** is light and falls mainly in the winter, giving an annual total of under 10 in (254mm), falling on only 36 days of the year. Average day time **temperatures** vary from 21°C (70°F) in January to 29°C (84°F) in August.

With the success of the port came new perils as it became the target of rival seafarers and pirates. Attacks came from Berbers, the Dutch and French Huguenots, but Santa Cruz's main problems came from English 'sea dogs' such as Drake, Hawkins and Blake. The most famous incident concerned the attack on Santa Cruz in 1797 by **Admiral Horatio Nelson**, who was ordered to raid the port and capture two ships loaded with bullion from Manila. Nelson's attack was a spectacular failure, as the defenders of the port had been forewarned of his supposedly surprise assault. In addition, rough seas scattered his flotilla of small landing boats. Many of Nelson's men were drowned, killed or wounded and the Admiral himself lost an arm in the battle. However, the victors were magnaminous and after treating Nelson's wounded sailors in the local hospital, they were returned to their ships with various gifts. The Admiral is said to have sent back English cheese and a keg of beer – which was a civilized ending to the fiasco. This was to be Nelson's only defeat in his glorious career.

In 1852, Queen Isabella II of Spain made Tenerife a **free trade zone** and Santa Cruz became a free port, which brought more prosperity to the city. However, as most

### GETTING TO SANTA CRUZ

In Santa Cruz, many travel agents offer **coach excursions**, usually described as 'shopping trips', to take advantage of the city's tax-free status. These are mainly half-day excursions as the shops close at 13:00. For visitors with a **hire car** a longer stay is possible, but the main problem is parking. It is best to arrive early and use the underground car park beneath the Plaza de España. A third option is to use the service **buses** which run half-hourly to Santa Cruz from Puerto de la Cruz and the main resorts in the south. Santa Cruz's bus station (*Estacion de Guaguas*) is near the Parque Marítimo, just a 10-minute walk to the city centre.

**Below:** *This craft shop in Santa Cruz also sells local costumes.*

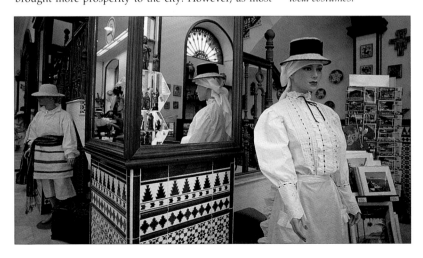

goods produced on Tenerife were exported through Santa Cruz, the port's trade reflected the island's 'boom and bust' economy as the monoculture in sugar cane, cochineal and bananas went through their cycles. The growth of tourism in the second half of the 20th century has only indirectly affected Santa Cruz, but the city has a busy, prosperous air and its port continues to thrive.

### THE HISTORIC CENTRE OF SANTA CRUZ
### Plaza de España ★★★

The hub of the city and an excellent place to start a walking tour is the **Plaza de España**. This square is relatively new, having been laid out in the 1940s on the site of the old San Cristóbal Castle. Numerous events take place in the square and in 1987, during the Carnival, Plaza de España claimed a place in the Guinness Book of Records, when over 200,000 people attended an open air dance here. The Plaza de España has several links with the Fascist era. In the centre of the square is the cruciform **Monumento de los Caídos** – the Monument to the Fallen in the Spanish Civil War (1936–39). There is a small memorial chapel in the base of the monument, from where a lift leads to the top, giving good views over the city and the harbour. Unfortunately the lift is usually closed because it became a target for Canarian separatists. To the southwest of the square are two rather severe looking buildings. The one nearest the harbour is the **Palacio Insular** (or Cabildo), identified by its clock tower. It mostly contains the offices of the island government. On the ground floor is the Tourist Office which can supply maps, brochures and accommodation information. It is also worth looking in the foyer of the Cabildo at the scale model of the island. Should

**Below:** *The Civil War monument dominates the bustling Plaza de España.*

the Tourist Office be closed, there is an information kiosk in the square. The other building is the Correos or post office. On the north side of the plaza are numerous cafés, the tables of which spill out onto the pavement.

**Above:** *Fine buildings and quality shops are to be found in the tree-lined Plaza de la Candelaria.*

### Plaza de la Candelaria ★★★

Leading off the Plaza de España is the much more attractive rectangular Plaza de la Candelaria. At the heart of the square is the Triunfo de la Candelaria, a monument in Carrera marble, carved by a Genoese sculptor. Topping the monument is a statue of the Madonna de la Candelaria, the patron saint of the islands. She carries, traditionally, a candle in her left hand and a baby in her right hand. Supporting the narrow obelisk are four Guanche chiefs, symbolically converted to Christianity. Amongst the fine buildings around the square are the Palacio de Carta which dates from 1752 and is now a bank (wander inside to see the fine patios) and the Casino de Tenerife, which is an exclusive gentlemen's club.

---

**THE PALACIO DE CARTA**

If you need to change a traveller's cheque in Santa Cruz, head for the Palacio de Carta, No. 9, in the Plaza de la Candelaria. The Palacio is occupied today by the Banco Español de Crédito and makes a fascinating location for financial transactions. It dates from 1752 and behind its rather drab façade lie a series of delightful patios, courtyards and balconies that can be appreciated during banking business hours.

**Above:** *The well-kept Parque García Sanabria, notable for its collection of plants and statues.*
**Opposite:** *The plain exterior of the Museo Militar conceals some fascinating displays.*

---

**THE REDUNDANT BULLRING**

There is a Plaza de Toros (bullring) in the north of the city, close to the Rambla de General Franco. Tourists wanting to see a bull fight will be out of luck. *Tintafeños* are not keen on bull fighting – a sentiment which forms part of their dismissive attitude towards mainland Spain. In any case, it would be far too expensive to import bulls and famous toreadors for just a few *corridas* a year. The bull-ring can, and is, put to other practical uses, such as typical Canary Island sports like stick fighting and wrestling.

---

## OTHER ATTRACTIVE SQUARES

Leading from the Plaza de la Candelaria is the pedestrianized Calle de Castillo, which is a shoppers' delight, full of stores and bazaars. This road leads to the **Plaza de General Weyler**, with its marble fountain, trees and sculptures. Along one side is the neoclassical building of the **Capitanía General**, erected by General Valeirano Weyler towards the end of the 19th century. The square suffers badly from traffic noise, so for a more peaceful spot turn right along Avenida del 25 de Julio and after 300m (328yd) the **Plaza de la Patos** is reached. In the centre of this attractive square is a tiled fountain notable for its large statues of green frogs squirting water towards an elegant swan. Around the fountain are a series of seats also composed of tiles, which were made in the famous Santa Ana factory in Seville. The plaza is lined with modernist buildings, mainly used for government offices. Further to the east is the **Plaza del Principe**, with a bandstand at its centre as well as numerous statues. Alongside the square is the **Museo Municipal de Bellas Artes**, or Fine Arts Museum (open 10:00–19:30, Monday to Friday). It mainly displays the paintings and sculptures of local artists, but also has collections of weapons, model ships and coins. Adjacent to the Fine Arts Museum is the **Iglesia de San Juzgados**

**Francísco**, which is said to have been founded by Irish monks fleeing from persecution in Elizabethan England. The present church, however, was once the chapel of a Franciscan friary.

## NORTH OF THE CITY CENTRE
### Parque Municipal García Sanabria ★★★

To escape from the bustle of the city, head for the **Parque Municipal García Sanabria**, located between the Rambla del General Franco and the Calle Méndez Nuñez. The park also operates as botanical gardens and is full of fountains, trees and promenades. It is notable for its fine collection of statues left over from the International Exhibition of Street Sculpture in 1973. More sculptures can be seen along the Rambla, including Henry Moore's *The Warrior.*

### Museo Militar de Almeyda ★★★

Where the Rambla meets the coastal Avenida de Anaga, you will see the **Museo Militar de Almeyda** (open 09:30–13:30, Tuesday to Sunday, admission free). This military museum is located in a 19th-century barracks. There are two main aspects to the museum. The first

---

**ANYONE FOR SHOPPING?**

With its duty-free status, Santa Cruz is a paradise for shoppers. The main shopping streets are the pedestrianized **Calle de Castillo** and the parallel **Calle Bethencourt Alfonso**. A feature of these streets is the Asian-owned bazaars, where you can try your hand at bargaining. Most shops and stores will accept Eurocheques and the major credit cards.

Another shopping spot worth visiting is the city market, the **Mercado de Nuestra Señora de Africa**. Here you can buy flowers, food, spices, cheeses and cheap, but dubious, electrical goods. If you are in Santa Cruz on a Sunday, do visit the **flea market** – held in the streets around the marketplace – where craft items, stamps, leatherware and general junk items are on sale.

### CARNIVAL

Santa Cruz's annual *Carnaval*, held for nine days just before Lent, is generally considered to be one of the best in the world, probably second only to the carnival in Rio de Janeiro. There is a different theme each year, shown to good effect in the numerous **processions**, or *comparsas*, with their floats and fantastic costumes. The colourful floats are accompanied by troupes of dancers, singers and musicians. Many visitors come from South America for the carnival and the streets echo to the sound of the rumba and samba – don't expect a good night's sleep during the festivities! The highlight of the Carnival is the election of the **carnival queen**. For this, the competitors wear elaborate costumes that can be as much as 3m (10ft) high and weigh anything up to 100kg (220lb). The carnival ends with a ceremony known as the **Burial of the Sardine**. A huge cardboard model of a sardine is carried through the streets to the waterfront where a 'funeral oration' takes place. The sardine is then burnt on a large bonfire, signalling the start of a fireworks display.

**Opposite:** *The bell tower of the Iglesia de Nuestra Señora de la Concepción rises above the city roofs.*
**Right:** *A flea market is held on Sundays in the streets around the Mercado.*

concerns General Franco, who spent four months in Tenerife as Commander General before leaving to conduct the Spanish Civil War. The other section inevitably deals with Nelson's botched attack on Santa Cruz in 1797. You can see the cannon called El Tigre (the tiger), which is supposed to have fired the shot that hit Nelson's right arm, which was later amputated. Before leaving the area, seek out the superb fountain in the museum's grounds.

### SOUTH OF THE CITY CENTRE

Three blocks southwest of the Plaza de España is the **Teatro Guimerá**, which is the home of the Tenerife Symphony Orchestra and used for theatre, opera and ballet performances. It was named after the dramatist Angel Guimerá, who, although born in Santa Cruz, did most of his work in Catalonia. The theatre, which dates from 1849, was built on the site of an old Dominican convent. Outside, there is an unusual statue in the form of a theatrical mask, which gives some curious optical effects.

Also to the south of the city centre, and close to the bus station and the sea shore, is the **Parque Marítimo**. This is a successful example of urban renewal in what was once a derelict dock area. The complex centres around the old **Castillo de San Juan** (Castle of St John) and consists of a large sea water lido designed by the late César Manrique, the famous architect and environmentalist from

Lanzarote. There are future plans for a maritime museum and other leisure facilities. Unfortunately, the nearby oil refinery spoils the atmosphere somewhat.

### Iglesia de Nuestra Señora de la Concepción ★★★
Approaching the dry river bed of the **Barranco de los Santos**, the six-tiered Moorish-looking tower of the **Iglesia de Nuestra Señora de la Concepción** comes into view. The octagonal turret on the top was used as a look-out point if pirates were expected. The original building was founded in 1502 by the Conquistadors, but it was badly damaged by fire in 1652 and underwent considerable restoration in the 17th and 18th centuries. There was further restoration in the 1990s and the church has only just re-opened. Apart from the tower, the exterior does not resemble a church at all and the visitor has to struggle to find the main entrance. The interior, however, is a gem. There are sturdy pillars of contrasting volcanic stone and a panelled Portuguese ceiling. There are the traditional five naves (the main nave and four large aisles) and ornately carved Canary wood choir stalls. Above the High Altar is the figure of the Mater Doloroso carved

---

**A NEW LANDMARK**

In the autumn of 2003 a startling new building was opened close to the Parque Maritimo on Santa Cruz's seafront. This is the **Auditorio de Tenerife**, a concert hall designed like a wave, and as distinctive a building as Sydney's Opera House. It was the work of the architect Santiago Calatrava, who also designed the airport in Bilbao, the train station in Lyon and the museum in Milwaukee. The Auditorio cost 75 million euros (£51 million) and most people in Tenerife consider the money well spent. It will be the home of the prestigious Tenerife Symphony Orchestra and there will be a full programme of opera, jazz, symphonic and chamber music for locals and tourists to enjoy.

**Right:** *Part of the curious collection of Guanche skulls in the Museo de la Naturaleza y el Hombre.*
**Opposite:** *Cars line up for the busy ferry in the port of Santa Cruz.*

---

**THE CHANGING PORT**

The port of Santa Cruz has been one of the busiest in Spain since the mid-1600s. Throughout its history it has been forced to adapt to changing trade demands and conditions. For centuries it was a staging post for goods, ships and passengers crossing the Atlantic, and had an important role in exporting the island's agricultural commodities such as bananas and sugar cane. Today, most goods are transported in containers. This has led to the growth of a large area of container docks alongside the coast road to the north-east of the port, marked by huge straddle carriers and other handling equipment. The port also provides facilities for a number of ferry boats, both from mainland Spain and from neighbouring islands. Large oil tankers from all over the world bring crude oil to the refinery south of the port. In recent years the biggest growth area in shipping has been with cruise liners, and Tenerife has proved a popular port of call for these vessels. In one day in 1999 the port held no fewer than five cruise liners with over 3000 passengers on board.

---

by Luján Pérez. To the left of the altar is the Chapel of the Holy Heart, which contains the Holy Cross carried by Alonso Fernández de Lugo when he first set foot on the island and which gave the city its name. To the right of the altar is the Carta Chapel. Note the *retablo*, which was carved on the order of Don Matías Carta. He died before it was completed and the skull and crossbones on the floor marks his tomb. His portrait is on the west wall of the chapel. It was painted after his death, as shown by the closed eyes and crossed arms. The church originally contained the English banners captured during Nelson's abortive raid, but these were transferred to the Military Museum during the recent renovations and are unlikely to be returned.

### Museo de la Naturaleza y el Hombre ★★★

Opposite the church on the other side of the Barranco de Santos, is the excellent **Museo de la Naturaleza y el Hombre** – the Museum of Nature and Man (open 10:00–20:00 daily, except Monday. Admission charge; free on Sundays). The museum was opened in 1997 in the old city hospital building. There is an excellent section on the flora and fauna of Tenerife, but most visitors will want to see the extensive archaeological section on the customs and art of the Guanches. There are over 1000 skulls on display, some showing the curious drilled holes for which the Guanches were well-known. There are also two mummies, one male and one female, and there is information on the mummification process. Not to be missed!

### Mercado de Nuestra Señora de Africa ★★★

A stone's throw from the museum is the city market, the **Mercado de Nuestra Señora de Africa**. Entry is through a large arch flanked by numerous flower stalls. Further in is a colourful collection of stalls selling fish, meat, fruit and vegetables, giving a genuine flavour of Tenerife life. On Sunday mornings there is a busy flea market in the surrounding streets.

---

**MUMMIFICATION**

One of the highlights of a visit to the Museo de la Naturaleza y el Hombre is the opportunity to see Guanche **mummies**. The Guanches mummified corpses in a similar but much cruder way to the ancient Egyptians. It appears that only the higher echelons of society were treated in this way. Intestines were removed from the bodies, which were then soaked in goats' milk and wrapped with reeds and animal skins. The bodies were then left in the sun to dry for around 14 days. This rather unpleasant work was carried out by lower-caste Guanches, who tended to be ostracized by society. The bodies were placed in remote, inaccessible caves, and it is for this reason that mummies are still being found today. It also appears that the mummified chiefs or *menceyes* were laid in wooden boxes which were then placed upright against the cave walls.

# Santa Cruz de Tenerife at a Glance

### BEST TIMES TO VISIT

Although Santa Cruz is located in the wetter north of the island, its coastal position means that it misses much of the cloud and rain that is found at some of the higher levels. From a climatic point of view, therefore, any time of the year is suitable for a visit to the capital. It does get extremely hot in summer, which some people might find rather trying.

### GETTING THERE

Public service **buses**, which are operated by the TITSA company, run a variety of routes to Santa Cruz from all parts of the island, and there are a number of regular shuttle buses that travel from from both of the airports. There are also tour groups that run **coach** excursions from all of the main resorts to Santa Cruz. Visitors who have **hire cars** will easily be able to reach the city from most of the main resorts within an hour's journey using the motorways.

### GETTING AROUND

Most of the main sights and attractions of Santa Cruz are within easy walking distance of the Plaza de España and are usually best visited on foot. **Taxis**, however, are cheap and plentiful, with a convenient taxi rank that is located right in the Plaza de España.

### WHERE TO STAY

Since Santa Cruz is not primarily a holiday resort, its hotels are mainly for business people.

#### *LUXURY*
**Mencey**, Calle José Naveiras 38, tel: 922 27 67 00, fax: 922 28 60 17.
This is the city's top hotel, luxuriously appointed and frequented by royalty, who no doubt appreciate the opulence of its Louis XIV style of furnishings.

#### *MID-RANGE*
**Atlantico**, Calle de Castillo 12, tel: 922 24 63 75, fax: 922 24 63 78.
This is a modern hotel, situated in a relatively quiet but very convenient part of the city centre.
**Taburiente**, Calle José Naveiras 24A, tel: 922 27 60 00, fax: 922 27 05 62. This well-appointed hotel is situated close to the municipal park. It also has a swimming pool.
**Contemporáneo**, Rambla del General Franco 116, tel: 922 27 15 71, fax: 922 28 00 17. This hotel offers bargain prices in a pleasant part of the city.

#### *BUDGET*
**Horizonte**, Calle Santa Rosa de Lima 11, tel: 922 27 19 36. This is a small, friendly and well-placed little hotel.

**Tanausu**, Calle Padre Anchieta 8, tel: 922 21 70 00, fax: 922 21 60 29. A small hotel in the south of Santa Cruz. It has no restaurant.

### WHERE TO EAT

Bear in mind that the restaurants in Santa Cruz cater mainly for the inhabitants of the capital and therefore the atmosphere and dress tend to be more restrained than in the resorts. There are some excellent snack bars with outside tables in the Plaza de la Candelaria and along the Rambla del General Franco.

#### *LUXURY*
**La Riviera**, Rambla del General Franco 155, tel: 922 27 58 12. Claims to serve the best food on the island.
**La Parilla**, Hotel Botánico, Avda. Richard Yeoward, tel: 922 38 14 00. High-class hotel restaurant serving international food.
**El Coto de Antonio**, Calle General Goded 13, tel: 922 27 21 05. Just off the Rambla and popular with the local business community.

#### *MID-RANGE*
**La Estancia**, Calle Mendez Nuñez 110, tel: 922 27 20 49. Head here for various local specialities.
**Mesón Los Monjes**, Calle La Marina 7, tel: 922 24 65 76. Centrally placed near the Plaza de España. Castilian decoration and recipes.

# Santa Cruz de Tenerife at a Glance

Many bars serve tapas or have a small dining room attached. Try one of these:

**Bar Cristobel**, Calle de la Rosa 75.

**Olympo**, Plaza de la Candelaria, tel: 922 24 17 38. Harbour views from terrace.

**Bar Mercado**, Calle de José Manuel Guimerá, next to the Sunday flea market.

### Tours and Excursions

Few excursions actually run from Santa Cruz as hardly any tourists stay in the city itself. However, there are a number of sights around Santa Cruz that are on the itinerary of many of the tour companies: these include the historic town of **La Laguna**, the **Museo de la Ciencia y el Cosmos** in La Laguna, the **Basilica** at **Candelaria** and the **Ethnographic Museum** and **Pyramids** at **Güimar**.

### Useful Contacts

**Tourist Information Centre:** Cabildo Insular de Tenerife, Plaza de España, tel: 922 60 55 92. Open Mon–Fri, 08:00– 18:00; Sat 09:00– 13:00. Helpful English-speaking staff, plenty of brochures available.

**Airports:**
**Los Rodeos Airport** (Tenerife North). For information, tel: 922 25 79 40; for bookings, tel: 922 28 80 00.

**Reina Sofía Airport** (Tenerife South). For information, tel: 922 77 00 50.

**Ferries:**
The **Fred Olsen Line** runs four ferries a day from Santa Cruz to Gran Canaria. Ferries run by **Trasmediterránea** leave once a week for Cádiz in mainland Spain, calling at Gran Canaria en route. Tickets for these ferries can be bought either at the Estación Marítima Muelle de Ribera on the quayside or from travel agents.

**Museo de la Naturaleza y el Hombre:**
Visitors wanting more detailed advice and information about any aspect of the archaeology, geology, marine biology or wildlife of the island can contact the curators of the Museo de la Naturaleza y el Hombre on the following telephone numbers:

**Archaeology**, tel: 922 20 93 17; **Natural Sciences**, tel: 922 22 87 53.
For **group visits**, tel: 922 20 93 14.

**Internet:**
You can use the e-mail facilities and also get onto the Internet at **Bar Ciber El Navegante**, Callejón del Combate 12.

**Walking:**
**Canarias Trekking**, tel/fax: 922 20 10 51, will organize hiking tours in many parts of the island.

**Consulates:**
The **British Consulate** is at Plaza Weyler 8 (on the first floor), tel: 922 28 68 63.
The **Irish Consulate** can be found at La Marina 7, tel: 922 24 56 71. The nearest **US Consulate** is on neighbouring Gran Canaria.

### Safety

Most crime against tourists on the island of Tenerife is of the petty variety, such as pick-pocketing, and does not involve violence against the person. Special care should be taken in Santa Cruz, how-ever – in common with most ports, the city has its seedy areas. Avoid these districts at night and take sensible precautions. Do not leave valuables on show in cars. Do not provide temptation for thieves by carrying handbags or leaving wallets in back pockets. Take par-ticular care at crowded places such as street markets and bus stations.

| SANTA CRUZ | J | F | M | A | M | J | J | A | S | O | N | D |
|---|---|---|---|---|---|---|---|---|---|---|---|---|
| AVERAGE TEMP. °F | 70 | 70 | 72 | 73 | 75 | 79 | 82 | 84 | 82 | 79 | 73 | 72 |
| AVERAGE TEMP. °C | 21 | 22 | 22 | 23 | 24 | 26 | 28 | 29 | 28 | 26 | 23 | 22 |
| HOURS OF SUN DAILY | 5 | 6 | 7 | 8 | 10 | 11 | 11 | 11 | 9 | 7 | 5 | 5 |
| RAINFALL in | 1.46 | 1.39 | 0.96 | 0.60 | 0.15 | 0.5 | 0 | 0.02 | 0.33 | 0.73 | 1.53 | 2 |
| RAINFALL mm | 37.3 | 35.5 | 24.3 | 15.2 | 3.8 | 1.3 | 0 | 0.6 | 8.5 | 18.5 | 38.9 | 51.0 |

# 3
# Northeast Tenerife

The peninsula in the northeast of Tenerife is geologically speaking the oldest part of the island. Although the rocks were formed from the lava flows of a volcano, the area has no evidence of recent volcanic activity. The area is dominated by the **Anaga Mountains** which are composed of basalt. Their jagged peaks rise to just over 1000m (3300ft) and their lower slopes are clothed with laurel and pine trees. This is also one of the wettest parts of Tenerife as the mountains are in the path of the rain-bearing **trade winds**. The cloud can be persistent, so visitors are advised to wait for a clear day before coming to the area. The Anaga Mountains are popular with walkers and numerous waymarked paths, which have survived since Guanche times, lead to remote villages such as **Chinamada** and **Chamorga**, where people still live in cave houses. The marvellous scenery can be appreciated from a number of **miradors**, or lookouts, which are to be found at intervals along the road that runs along the spine of the range.

The gateway to the Anaga Mountains is the ancient city of **La Laguna**. Once the capital of Tenerife, it is an ecclesiastic centre with the island's only cathedral and a number of monasteries and convents. La Laguna is also the home of the only traditional university in the Canary Islands. Despite its attractions, the city sees few visitors and is largely ignored by tour operators and coach firms.

The eastern and western coasts present striking contrasts. On the more arid east coast the main attraction is the artificial beach of **Playa de las Teresitas**, the golden

**DON'T MISS**

*** Historic La Laguna:** full of mansions, palaces, churches and convents.
** The Anaga Mountains:** jagged, forested mountains with good viewpoints.
** Playa de las Teresitas:** a golden beach composed of sand brought from the Sahara Desert.
** Casa de Carta:** the finest ethnographic museum in the Canary Islands.
** Casa del Vino *La Baranda*:** popular wine museum and restaurant.

**Opposite:** *The sweep of the artificial Teresitas beach, with the village of San Andrés in the background.*

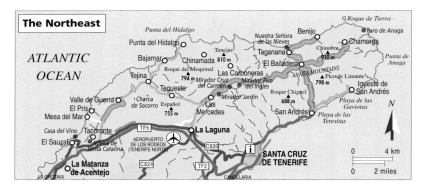

sand of which was transported from the Sahara Desert. The western coast is lower lying and fertile, making it good farming country. Grapes grow particularly well in the area around **Tacoronte**. Don't miss the **Casa del Vino** *La Baranda*, a wine museum just outside the town. Near to Tacoronte is the pretty village of **El Sauzal**. Its white-domed church is one of the most photographed sights on the island.

The northwest coast also has a number of small holiday resorts, including **Mesa del Mar**. Further to the north are some larger resorts, such as **Bajamar** and **Punta del Hidalgo**, which are both popular with German visitors. This stretch of coast is mountainous and rocky, with rough seas, which means that swimming is safer in hotel pools.

### San Andrés and Playa de las Teresitas ★★

The road northeast out of Santa Cruz passes along several kilometres of docks with towering container handling equipment, the Club Nautico and the occasional cruise liner, before reaching the attractive fishing village of **San Andrés**. Here the white houses straggle up the hillside, interspersed with pretty squares. Down at sea level, a number of excellent fish restaurants line the main road. A ruined fort can be seen on the northeastern outskirts of the village. It was constructed in the 18th century by Captain General Agustín de Robles. Just to the north, a crescent of

---

**CLIMATE**

Northeast Tenerife is the wettest part of the island, as the Anaga Mountains lie right in the path of the rain-bearing trade winds. Most rain falls in the **winter** and amounts are sufficient for sub tropical crops to be grown without irrigation. The moist winds frequently form a persistent **cloud** layer between 500m (1650ft) and 1500m (4900ft), keeping temperatures lower than on the coasts. Although there is less cloud and rain in the summer, precipitation can be expected at any time of the year.

golden sand marks the **Playa de las Teresitas**, a popular weekend venue for the inhabitants of Santa Cruz. Tenerife has few good beaches – they are mainly composed of boulders or black volcanic sand – but Playa de las Teresitas is undoubtedly the best. The beach, however, is entirely artificial – it is made up of over 4 million sacks of sand that were shipped in from the Sahara in the mid-1970s. A man-made stone reef protects the beach from storm waves and ensures safe swimming. The 2km (1-mile) long beach has plenty of facilities, including shady palm trees, beach bars, pedaloes and a windsurfing school. The land behind the beach has so far resisted development, but this situation will probably not last for long, as some 30 proposals for projects have been received by the authorities, from local, national and international groups. The coast road continues as far as the picturesque village of Igueste. Halfway along the road is the quiet beach of **Playa de las Gaviotas**, which is popular with nudists. The road winds its way up to the Punta de los Organos, where a mirador gives stunning views all along the coast as far as Candelaria.

### HEADING INLAND

The road from San Andrés into the interior leaves the arid coastline and heads into the mountains with a series of hairpin bends. The vegetation is more luxuriant and the laurel and pine forests hold declining populations of the endangered Bolle's and white-tailed laurel pigeons.

---

**ENDANGERED PIGEONS**

The laurel forests of the Anaga Mountains are home to two members of the pigeon family that are on the list of endangered species. They are the **Bolles laurel pigeon** and the **white-tailed laurel pigeon**. They are found only on Tenerife and the smaller islands of La Palma, El Hierro and La Gomera. The pigeons feed largely on laurel berries and lay only one egg in a nest in the lush vegetation that the laurel trees supply. Over the last two centuries the laurel forests have disappeared at an alarming rate to make way for agriculture, depriving the pigeons of their vital habitat.

---

**Left:** *Playa de las Teresitas is composed of artificial sand brought from the Sahara Desert.*

**Below:** *The remains of cave houses are common in the Anaga Mountains.*

### El Bailadero ★★★

At the spine of the mountains the hamlet of **El Bailadero** is reached. The name comes from an old Guanche word, *baladero*, meaning 'bleating place'. It was here that the Guanches would bring their sheep in the hope that their bleating would persuade the gods to bring rain.

From El Bailadero there is a choice of routes. To the right a rough road leads to the remote hamlet of **Chamorga**, from whence footpaths lead down through the tiny settlement of Casas Blancas to the sea and Tenerife's most northerly lighthouse, the Faro de Anaga. The second route from El Bailadero runs northwards through a tunnel and then drops down along more hair-pin bends to the white village of **Taganana**, which dates back to the early 16th century. It is worth stopping to look at the village church of Nuestra Señora de las Nieves (Our Lady of the Snows), one of the oldest on the island. If you can gain entry, don't miss the superb Flemish triptych, believed to date from the early 1500s. Taganana was once an important centre for the production of sugar and it is still a thriving agricultural centre with crops grown on its terraced hill slopes. The road continues along the shore to the small, rocky beaches of **San Roque**, **Almaciga** and **Benijo**, notable for their contorted rocks and sea caves. The road soon peters out, but a footpath continues around the headland to the lighthouse.

Back at El Bailadero, the main route runs westwards along the spine of the mountains, with a series of miradors giving marvellous views in all directions. The first is the **Mirador Pico del Inglés**, said to

**Above:** *A house is the subject of this charming wall decoration in La Laguna.*

be named after an Englishman who walked all the way here from La Laguna in a day. The views can be stupendous and on a clear day it is possible to see Mount Teide and even Gran Canaria. A rough road leads from the mirador to the remote village of **Las Carboneras**. From here, tracks can be followed to the hamlet of **Chinamada**, where the 30 or so inhabitants still live in cave houses. If you can look inside one of them you will find, however, that the interiors are far removed from the Stone Age (*see* panel, page 55). From the Mirador Pico del Inglés, the road continues west to **Las Mercedes**, where you find the **Mirador Cruz del Carmen**. Here there is a new Visitors' Centre, picnic area and restaurant. A viewing platform looks down over the dense laurel forest. There is also a small chapel containing the statue of Nuestra Señora de los Mercedes. Lastly, there is the **Mirador Jardín**, which gives fine views westward over La Laguna and across the Aguere valley towards Mount Teide.

## La Laguna ★★★

The city of **San Cristóbal de la Laguna** is the oldest settlement on the island of Tenerife. It was founded by Alfonso Fernández de Lugo after he had conquered the island in 1496, having defeated the Guanches at this spot. It remained the capital until it was superceded by Santa Cruz in 1723. La Laguna lies in a broad valley some 550m (1800ft) above sea level, where the climate is cooler than on the coast. It gains its name from a small lagoon that was drained in 1837, filled in and built over. Today, La

### CIGAR MAKING CITY

The fact that many of the inhabitants of Tenerife have emigrated to Cuba and later returned may explain why the manufacture of cigars takes place in a number of towns on the island. The warm, sub tropical climate, suits the cultivation of the tobacco plant, particularly near La Laguna, where there is an important cigar-making industry. The city is especially known for the hand made *palmero*, rolled within an individual leaf.

La Laguna

Laguna is a city of contrasts. To the north of the commercial and shopping centre is the old part of the city – the *casco histórico*, largely responsible for the decision in 2000 to include La Laguna on UNESCO's World Heritage List. This area retains its original street plan laid out in a grid system. It is full of historical stone buildings, with wooden balconies and flower-filled patios. The old city's ecclesiastical importance is shown by its cathedral and a wealth of churches, monasteries and convents. To the south of the town centre you will find the modern university area, with the associated Astrophysics Institute and Museum of Science and Technology. Strangely, La Laguna sees relatively few tourists – a situation with which the local authorities seem quite happy. However, La Laguna can easily be reached via the motorway system and the historical quarter is one of the gems of the island.

### Historical La Laguna

The best starting point for a walk around the historical area is in the **Plaza del Adelantado**. This shady square, with its central marble fountain, is surrounded by ancient buildings of interest. On the eastern side are the market, the law courts and the **Ermita San Miguel**, a monastery that dates back to the early 16th century. On the south side of the square is the **Birthplace of Father Anchieta**, the missionary who founded the city of São Paulo in Brazil, and the neoclassical **Ayuntamiento** (Town Hall), which was built in 1822. Another striking building is the **Palacio de Nava** which dates from 1590

## PADRE ANCHIETA

Visitors leaving the motorway to enter La Laguna will notice a large statue near the intersection. This is a sculpture of Padre José de Anchieta, a gift from the Brazilian government. Anchieta was born in La Laguna in 1534 and studied in Portugal. He then became a Jesuit missionary. He spent much of his life in Brazil where he took a special interest in the way of life of the indigenous tribes. Anchieta is believed to have converted more than two million South American natives to Christianity. He also founded the Brazilian city of São Paolo, now one of the largest in the world. Padre Anchieta died in Brazil in 1597.

and has a façade which shows a variety of architectural styles, including Baroque and neoclassical. The whole of one side of the plaza is taken up with the **Convent of Santa Catalina de Sienna**. It was set up in the 17th century and still has a community of cloistered nuns. Note the superb *ajimeces*, or enclosed wooden balconies. The convent's church has an impressive panelled *Mudéjar* ceiling and an unusual wood and silver altarpiece. The convent is open on 15 February each year for people to see the incorruptible body of María de Jesús, to whom miracles have been attributed.

### Museo de Historia de Tenerife ★★★

Leave the Plaza del Adelantado on the north side along Calle de Nava y Grimón and then turn left into Calle San Agustín. Shortly on the right is the **Museo de Historia de Tenerife**, located in the Casa Lercaro, a fine 16th-century townhouse. Undoubtedly the best history museum in the Canary Islands, it traces the history of Tenerife from the Spanish Conquest to the present day and has a particularly good map collection (open Tue–Sat 10:00–17:00, Sun 10:00–14:00, small admission charge). Next door to the museum is the **Palacio Episcopal**, an early 17th-century building which was a casino before it became a bishop's palace.

### Iglesia de Nuestra Señora de la Concepción ★★★

At the end of Calle San Agustín, turn left and arrive at the Plaza de la Concepción, where you'll find La Laguna's oldest church, and the oldest parish church on the island, the **Iglesia de Nuestra Señora de la Concepción**. It dates from the early years of the 16th century, but much of its early architecture has been swamped by the later Gothic, Renaissance and Baroque additions. The church's most distinctive feature is its Moorish looking seven-tiered tower. Inside there is a fine *Mudéjar* ceiling, an 18th-century cedarwood pulpit and some beautifully carved

> **LA LAGUNA'S UNIVERSITY**
>
> Until very recently, the university at La Laguna was the only such institution in the Canary Islands. It was founded in the early 18th century by the Augustinians and the original building was in Calle San Agustín in the old part of the city. A new campus was built in the 1950s on the south side of La Laguna. There are nearly 13,000 students, who certainly add to the vibrant atmosphere in the city. A second university has now been set up in Gran Canaria to cope with the demand in the archipelago.

**Below:** *Lofty church spires reflect La Laguna's importance as a religious centre.*

### THE CASA DEL VINO

A popular new tourist attraction in northeast Tenerife is the Casa del Vino *La Baranda*. It is located in a 17th-century house between El Sauzal and Tacoronte. There is a small museum and a video presentation describing the history of wine making in Tenerife. Visitors can sample a selection of the wines of the area and buy bottles of their choice. The Casa del Vino also has an excellent restaurant, where diners can eat on a terrace with splendid views along the coastline.

choir stalls. There are also sculptures by Pérez and Estévez and some ornate *retablos*. One of the statues, that of San Juan Evangelista, is said to have begun to sweat on 6 May 1648, and continued to do so for 40 days. Nobody has produced a scientific explanation for this 'miracle'. In the baptistery at the side of the church is a font, made of Seville ceramics; there are claims that it was used to baptize the Guanche leaders. The church is usually open Mon–Fri, 10:00–12:00, and during services.

### Cathedral ★★★

A return to the Plaza del Adelantado via Calle del Obispo Rey Redondo passes the **Cathedral**, located in a small square graced by lofty palms. Tenerife's only cathedral dates back to 1515, and for many years it was the parish church of Los Remedios. When the bishopric was created in 1818, the church was upgraded to a cathedral and a considerable amount of work was carried out, including the construction of a classical façade. The interior is rather gloomy, but it is worth seeking out the statues by Luján Pérez and also the grave of Alonso Fernández de Lujo, which can be found behind the high altar.

### Iglesia de San Francisco ★★★

Another excursion north from the Plaza del Adelantado leads via Calle de Nava y Grimón to the impressive

**Opposite:** *The simple little church of San Pedro at El Sauzal, with its photogenic white dome.*
**Right:** *A huge satellite dish at the hi-tech Museo de la Ciencia y del Cosmos.*

Plaza de San Francisco, where the main attraction is the **Iglesia de San Francisco**. In the sanctuary is the statue of Christ, the *Santísimo Cristo de la Laguna*, which is believed to have been brought to Tenerife by Alonso Fernández de Lugo in 1520. The figure was carved in black oak from Flanders by a Sevillian

sculptor. The statue, which is one of the most venerated in the Canary Islands, is brought out at Easter to lead the Holy Week processions.

### The University Area ★★★

The modern part of La Laguna lies to the south of the city centre and is based around the **University**. The 13,000 or so students create a lively atmosphere in the city. Associated with the university is the **Canarian Astrophysics Institute**, which also runs observatories on Mount Teide and on the island of La Palma. Also owned by the university is the fascinating **Museo de la Ciencia y del Cosmos** (Museum of Science and the Cosmos), which is noted for its hands-on, hi-tech presentation. Amongst other things you can undertake a lie detector test, experience the sound heard by a foetus in its mother's womb, communicate with outer space, pass through a maze of mirrors and even see your own skeleton!

### THE WEST OF THE REGION

There are a number of small towns in the west of the region that are worth a visit, including Tacoronte, El Sauzal, Tegueste and Tejina, to name just a few. Here the Anaga Mountains slope gently westward and the volcanic soil and the moist conditions provide excellent conditions for agriculture.

---

**THE TROGLODYTE TENDENCY**

That some of the inhabitants of Tenerife still live in caves would surprise many visitors. This fact is true, but not as simple as it first seems. In the village of **Chinamada** in a remote part of the Anaga Mountains, there are some 30 families living in 'cave houses'. From the outside they look like normal houses, but closer inspection shows that behind the windows and doors, the rest of the house extends back into the rocky hillside. There may, in fact, be several cave rooms and small chimneys may be detected above, taking away the smoke from fires and kitchens. Although no electricity has reached Chinamada, the use of batteries, bottled gas and even solar panels, means that the residents have all the mod cons required for 21st-century living. The caves also have their own natural form of air conditioning, with the temperatures remaining constant throughout the year.

### Tacoronte ★★★

**Tacoronte** is an important market town of around 17,000 inhabitants. It is believed to have gained its name from the Guanche word *tagoro*, which means 'meeting place'. Potatoes and other vegetables are produced around here, but the town is most famous for its wine. In this part of the country vines can be grown without irrigation and Tacoronte wines were the first in the Canary Islands to be granted a DOC (certificate of origin). Particularly well-known are their strong sherry-like Malvesia wines. Tacoronte also possesses two interesting churches, close to each other in the town centre. The **Iglesia de Santa Catalina** dates back to 1664 and has a distinctive black and white bell tower. The **Iglesia del Cristo de los Dolores** was once part of an Augustinian monastery. Look for its altar of Mexican silver and the superb coffered ceiling panels. The fiesta of Cristo de los Dolores in September celebrates the wine harvest.

### El Sauzal ★★★

Another nearby town in the wine-producing area is **El Sauzal**, its name derived from the willow trees, or *sauces*, that grow in the vicinity. El Sauzal is located on the top of a steep 300m (985ft) cliff overlooking the Atlantic – head for the Mirador de la Garañona which gives spectacular views along the coastline. Another sight in El Sauzal which should not be missed is the **Iglesia de San Pedro**, notable for its Moorish-style white dome. A photograph of the church, with a snow-capped Mount Teide in the distance, can look stunning. A visit to the Botanical Gardens *Las Tosquillas* is also recommended. Set up in 1957, the gardens cover some 5000m$^2$ (5980 sq yd). There are 50 species of palms from all over the world and a unique collection of 80 different types of air carnations or Tillandsias. Free-flying parrots and cockatoos add to the ambience. Wine buffs will head for the **Casa del Vino** *La Baranda* located in a typical 17th-century farmhouse. An exhibition shows the history of wine-making on Tenerife. Wines can be tasted and bought from the gift shop, which also sells wine-related articles (closed Mondays).

Just north of El Sauzal are the two coastal hamlets of **Mesa del Mar** and **El Pris**, which are reached by steep roads. Both have good fish restaurants.

### Valle de Guerra ★★★

The road north of El Sauzal heads inland to the town of **Valle de Guerra**, which is surrounded by rich agricultural land producing bananas and cut flowers such as strelitzia. The main reason for coming here, however, is to visit the **Casa de Carta Ethnographic Museum**. It is located in a well-restored 17th-century mansion and is without doubt the best museum of its type in the Canary Islands. The house itself is superb, with courtyards, balconies and patios providing wonderful views of the surrounding countryside. The displays present Canarian rural life over the centuries, with examples of country crafts and historic equipment. Particularly impressive are the folk costumes from various parts of Tenerife and the other islands. The museum is open Tue–Sat, 10:00–20:00.

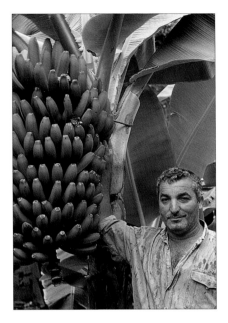

**Above:** *Banana production flourishes on Tenerife, particularly around the town of Valle de Guerra.*

### Tegueste and Tejina ★★★

Just off the road to the north is the small town of **Tegueste**. This is another wine producing area and the gateway to some good walking country in the lower slopes of the Anaga Mountains. Tegueste's main claim to fame is that it has the best Canarian wrestling team on the island. It also has one the most important *romerias* in Tenerife, when horse-drawn carts are decorated with fruit and vegetables. Nearby **Tejina**, on the eastern side of the Valle de Guerra, was once an important town for the production of sugar cane. This led to a local rum-making industry. The factory still operates, but the sugar cane is now imported from other countries.

**Above:** *The promenade in the quiet resort of Bajamar in the north of Tenerife.*

### LOW-KEY HOLIDAY RESORTS

The road now swings towards the coast arriving first at **Bajamar** (the name literally means 'down by the sea'). It has a marvellous position on a platform between the foothills of the Anaga Mountains and the sea cliffs. Bajamar was one of the earliest resorts to develop in Tenerife, but it suffers from a lack of a good beach and experiences strong winds and waves. As a result it cannot compete with the big resorts in the south and has remained fairly low key. However, many visitors, particularly mainland Spaniards and Germans, like the quiet atmosphere and return time and again. The same is true of the last resort along the coast road, **Punta del Hidalgo**, where there has been rather more high-rise development. The fierce winds mean that most swimming has to take place in hotel pools. There are good views of the Anaga Mountains, particularly the twin peaks of **Roque Dos Hermanos**. There is a well-marked footpath from Punta del Hidalgo leading up to the cave village of **Chinamada** – allow three hours for the ascent.

# Northeast Tenerife at a Glance

## BEST TIMES TO VISIT

The northeast of Tenerife can be visited throughout the year. The winter is cloudier than the summer, particularly in the Anaga Mountains, which faces the rain-bearing trade winds. Because of this it is important that you choose a clear day on which to visit the mountains, whatever time of year, as there are many wonderful views that will be missed under cloud cover.

## GETTING THERE

TITSA **buses** run regularly from both Santa Cruz and Puerto de la Cruz to the main towns of the northeastern parts of Tenerife.

## GETTING AROUND

Although TITSA buses link the main towns of the northeast, the service can be patchy and infrequent. Many of the smaller villages have no bus connections at all. **Car hire** is clearly the best option for seeing the main sights of the area and getting to the more remote parts. In some areas there are still a few isolated villages that can only be reached on foot or by use of off-road vehicles. Those without a car may have to resort to **taxis**, in view of the scarcity of buses.

## WHERE TO STAY

In many parts of the northeast of Tenerife, there is little choice of accommodation.

The best possibilities are in La Laguna and in the small holiday resorts on the north-west coast.

## MID-RANGE

**Delfin**, Avenida del Sol, Bajamar, tel: 922 54 02 00, fax: 922 54 02 00. This modern hotel is situated near the sea. It has a pool and tennis courts.
**Neptuno**, Calle Punta Hidalgo, Bajamar, tel: 922 54 25 62. This hotel has two pools as well as excellent mountain views.
**Nivaria**, Plaza del Adelantado 11, tel: 922 26 42 95, fax: 922 25 96 34. This is a good location for those wishing to explore the old town of La Laguna.

## BUDGET

**Nautilus**, Avenida de las Piscinas 2, Bajamar, tel: 922 54 05 00. This is a small but comfortable hotel with all the basic facilities.
**Aguere**, Calle Obispo Rey Redondo 57, La Laguna, tel: 922 25 94 90, fax: 922 63 16 33. This small hotel is situated in the heart of the old town of La Laguna.

## WHERE TO EAT

Although good restaurants are quite hard to find in the more remote rural areas, there is still plenty of choice in La Laguna and the north-west resorts.

## MID-RANGE

**La Hoya del Camillo**, Ctra. General del Norte 118, La Laguna, tel: 922 26 20 54. This is probably La Laguna's best restaurant.
**San Nicholas**, Ctra. General de Sauzal, El Sauzal. Excellent fish restaurant.
**Restaurante San Antonio**, Plaza de San Francisco 6, La Laguna. Atmospheric court-yard eating.
**Casa del Vino**, restaurant of the Wine Museum, La Baranda, El Sauzal, tel: 922 57 25 35. Terrace with sea view.

## BUDGET

La Laguna has some excellent tapas bars, including:
**Tasca La Laguna**, Calle de Juan de Vera 53; **Tasca Lagunera**, Plaza Dr. Regulo 6 and **Tasca La Panadería**, Calle de San Domingo 24.

## TOURS AND EXCURSIONS

The two most popular excursions in the area are to the **Casa de Carta Ethnographic Museum** near Valle de Guerra and the **Casa del Vino la Baranda** near El Sauzal.

## USEFUL CONTACTS

**Tourist Information Centre**, Ayuntamiento, Plaza del Adelantado, La Laguna. There is a kiosk in the square, open 08:30–19:00 daily.
For **horse riding**, contact El Molino, tel: 922 54 16 58 (at Tegueste), or Atalaya, tel: 922 25 57 39 (at La Laguna).

# 4
# The Northern Coast

The northern coastal area of Tenerife is undoubtedly the most attractive part of the island. The trade winds ensure that it is cloudier and wetter than the arid south of the island, but these conditions encourage prolific vegetation and the growth of subtropical crops such as bananas and oranges. In the centre of the region is Tenerife's second most important town of **Puerto de la Cruz**. It became the prime port on the north coast of the island after the destruction of Garachico by volcanic activity, but the heavy Atlantic swell and the lack of shelter meant that it soon lost business to Santa Cruz. Fortunately, Puerto then developed as Tenerife's first holiday resort. Despite the cloudy weather, particularly in winter, it attracts more tourists than any other resort. Theme parks, such as **Loro Parque** and **Bananera el Guanche** are close by.

You can also visit the dignified old town of **La Orotava**, located on a broad, upland valley. It is noted for the colonial architecture of its houses and public buildings, with their flower-bedecked wooden balconies and shady courtyards. La Orotava is also famous for its 'flower carpets' at Corpus Christi. In the east of the area are the twin towns of **La Matanza de Acentejo** and **La Victoria de Acentejo**, the sites of battles between the troops of Alfonso Fernández de Lugo and the Guanche army in the 15th century.

To the west of Puerto Cruz is the well-known wine-producing area based around **Icod de los Vinos**, a town which is also famous for its venerable **Dragon tree**, claimed to be the oldest on the island. Nearby is the coastal town of **Garachico**, once Tenerife's largest port until volcanic lava

## DON'T MISS

**\*\*\* Loro Parque:** most popular theme park.
**\*\* Las Casas de los Balcones:** craft centre with traditional Canarian architecture in La Orotava.
**\*\* Lido San Telmo:** Puerto de la Cruz's seafront complex of pools.
**\* The Dragon Tree at Icod:** Over 1000 years old.
**\* Jardín Botánico:** Puerto's Botanical Gardens.
**\* The 'Flower Carpets' at La Orotava:** designs made of volcanic sand and flowers at the Corpus Christi festival.

**Opposite:** *Lido San Telmo in Puerto de la Cruz was designed by César Manrique.*

**Puerto de la Cruz**

engulfed the settlement in 1706. The peninsula to the west was once remote and saw few tourists, but this is gradually changing as the attractions of villages such as **Masca** and **Buenavista del Norte** become more obvious.

The north coast provides some easy routes to Tenerife's main attraction, the volcanic mountain of **Mount Teide**, whose snow-capped peak looms over the region, providing endless photographic opportunities.

## PUERTO DE LA CRUZ

Located at the northern end of the Orotava Valley, Puerto de la Cruz (or Puerto as it is more simply known) was founded in the early 17th century, when Philip IV selected it to be the main port of the district. It briefly increased in importance when a volcanic eruption and subsequent lava flow closed the rival port of Garachico to the west. However, the rocky coastline, Atlantic swell and the lack of a sheltered harbour, meant that its development would always be limited and it soon lost its influence to Santa Cruz in the east of the island.

By the late 19th century, Puerto de la Cruz was developing as a tourist centre as wealthy Victorian visitors from England stopped off on the voyage back from overseas. The British built the first hotels, such as the Taoro (which is now a casino) and the Monopol in the Plaza de Iglesia. The main development was to come in the 1960s, when charter flights began to bring tourists in large numbers. The more unsightly hotels and apartment blocks along the sea front at Puerto date from this time. The growth of resorts such as Los Cristianos and Playa de las Américas in the south of the island in the 1980s and 1990s provided new attractions for younger visitors.

### Sights and Attractions ***

The hub of all the activity in Puerto de la Cruz is the **Plaza de Charco de los Camarones** (the Square of the Shrimp Pool), which was named after a tidal lagoon where the locals used to dredge for shrimps. Now raised and dry, the Plaza is shaded by massive Indian laurels and palm trees, the home of noisy feral parakeets. It is the haunt of shoe-shine boys, lottery ticket sellers and those with enough time for a game of outdoor chess. In the streets around the square are numerous Indian bazaars selling a range of bargain goods. The Plaza del Charco is also the site of the town's main taxi rank. Just off the Plaza is the **Museo Arqueológico** located in a 19th-century mansion. This small museum has a modest collection of remains from Guanche times, including a few mummies. Open 10:00–13:00 and 17:00–21:00, Tue–Sat; 10:00–13:00 Sun.

Leave the Plaza de Charco eastwards via the Calle de Quintana. On the left is the tiny **Ermita de San Juan**, which dates from the early years of the 17th century. The Calle de Quintana links up with Puerto's other attractive square, the more peaceful **Plaza de la Iglesia**. Dominating the square is the **Iglesia de Nuestra Señora de la Peña**

---

**TWO SONS OF PUERTO**

In the Plaza de la Iglesia in Puerto de la Cruz is a bust of **Agustín de Béthancourt** who was born in the town in 1798. After qualifying as an engineer, he spent much of his life in Russia, where he became a general in the army, in charge of building bridges, canals and roads. Another famous son of Puerto was **Tómas de Iriarte**, who was born in 1750. He moved to Madrid in his teens and quickly became famous as a writer and playwright. His writing usually had a strong social comment. His birthplace is now a small museum. Both Béthancourt and Iriarte have streets in Puerto de la Cruz named after them.

**Below:** *The beautiful coastline at Puerto de la Cruz brings visitors back year after year.*

**Below:** *The Jardín Botánico was set up by Carlos III in 1788 as an acclimatization site for tropical plants.*

de Francia (Church of Our Lady of the Rock of France). The church was built between 1684 and 1697, with the tower added in 1898. The somewhat gloomy interior has a number of items of interest, including a *Mudéjar* ceiling, paintings by Luis de la Cruz, carvings by José Luján Pérez and an organ brought from London in 1814. Note, too, in a side chapel, the statue of the Virgen del Carmen, which is carried at the head of the fishermen's procession each July. Outside the church, in the shady plaza is a delightful swan fountain and a statue of Agustín de Béthancourt, the engineer who was a native of Puerto de la Cruz. On the north side of the square are the town's oldest hotels, the **Hotel Marquesa**, which dates from 1712 and the **Hotel Monopol**, which was built in 1742. Both have attractive wooden balconies and courtyards. Just off the plaza, in Calle Iriarte is **Casa Iriarte**, the birthplace of the writer Tomás de Iriarte. This 18th-century house has some carved balconies and an attractive patio, but unfortunately the rather hotchpotch 'naval' museum on the upper floor and the souvenir shop on the ground floor do nothing to enhance one of the town's finest houses.

Most of the other attractions of Puerto are situated along the seafront. In the west is the **Playa Jardín**, a man-made beach backed by superb tropical gardens complete with sculptures. Nearby is the **Castillo de San Felipe**, all that remains of a line of defensive fortifications that once protected the port. The castle is now used for exhibitions and concerts. Further to the east is the **Puerto Pesquero**, or fishermen's harbour, a small-scale affair with a few token

boats hauled up on a tiny shingle beach. There are some ancient buildings in this area, including the **Casa de Real Aduana** (the Royal Customs House) dating from 1620 and built in the traditional black and white stone. It was a working customs house until 1833. Opposite is the **Casa**

**Miranda**, once the 18th-century home of Francisco de Miranda, who was prominent in Venezuela's fight for independence. The building is now a restaurant.

Past the modern Plaza de Europa, the promenade known as Calle del San Telmo leads to the **Ermita de San Telmo**. This small chapel was founded by sailors in 1626 and dedicated to St Elmo, patron saint of seafarers. It has few treasures, but its simplicity never fails to impress. Just past the chapel is the **Lido San Telmo** (also known as the Costa Martiánez). Designed by the Lanzarote architect, artist and environmentalist, César Manrique, in 1977, the Lido is a complex of pools, islands of volcanic rock, lawns and shrubbery. Beneath the complex is the **Sala Andrómeda**, claimed to be the only subaquatic nightclub in the world. There is a small entrance fee to the Lido.

**Above** *The Lido San Telmo, also known as the Costa Martiánez, occupies a large stretch of the seafront.*

### On the Higher Land to the South ★★★

As the low-lying land around the old port became entirely built over, developments took place in the **Mount Taoro** area on higher land to the south. In 1882, the Grand Hotel Taoro was built and for many years it was the most prestigious hotel in the Canary Islands. It is now best known for its **Casino**, where roulette, blackjack and slot machines can be played. Formal dress is required, along with a passport. Adjacent to the Casino are the attractive ornamental gardens of the **Parque Taoro** and the aquatic gardens of the **Risco Bello Jardín Aquático**.

By far the most interesting garden, however, is the **Jardín Botánico**. The official name of this 2.5ha (6-acre) walled garden is La Orotava Acclimatization Garden. It was set up in 1788 by King Carlos III of Spain as a sort of halfway house for tropical plants to acclimatize before being sent on to mainland Spain. Few plants, in fact, survived the Spanish winters, but the acclimatization garden remains one of the main attractions of Tenerife. There are over 4000 plants here, including a massive 200-year-old

---

**CÉSAR MANRIQUE**

The impressive **Lido San Telmo** in Puerto de la Cruz was the work of César Manrique, the artist, sculptor, architect and environmentalist, who was born on Lanzarote in 1919. After establishing a reputation as a painter, he devoted much of his life to saving the Canary Islands from the worst excesses of mass tourism, particularly in the field of architecture. His essential approach was that buildings should always be in harmony with the natural landscape around them. He also designed the **Playa Jardín** in Puerto de la Cruz, the **Parque Marítimo** in Santa Cruz and the **Mirador del Palmarejo** on the island of La Gomera. Manrique, sadly, died in a car crash in 1992.

South American rubber tree, scores of orchids and other exotics. Visitors will also enjoy the feral parrots that nest here and the ornamental pond which is the centrepiece of the gardens. Open daily, 09:00–18:00.

### Theme Parks ★★★

Visitors to Puerto de la Cruz, and indeed the whole of Tenerife, have two excellent theme parks to enjoy. On the western edge of the town is **Loro Parque** (Parrot Park). It was opened in 1982 and now has the largest collection of parrots, macaws, parakeets and similar species in the world. The park seems to expand annually and in addition to the parrots there is a dolphinarium, an aquarium with a walk-through plastic tunnel allowing eye to eye contact with sharks and rays, flamingo pools, a bat colony, monkey house and a Thai village – all set in superbly landscaped grounds. The latest attraction for the millennium is 'planet penguin' – an environment created for penguins in what has been described as 'the world's largest refrigerator'. Loro Parque has, not surprisingly, proved to be the most popular tourist attraction in the Canary Islands. The park can be reached by a free road train from the centre of Puerto de la Cruz. Open daily, 08:30–18:45; last admission 17:00.

The other local attraction is **Bananera el Guanche** just off the autopista to the east of the town. This is a working banana plantation where visitors are given a video introduction explaining the history of the banana trade. They can then follow waymarked paths on a self-guided tour through the plantation. There are not only bananas, but other exotic fruits, such as mangoes, pineapples, pawpaws, grapefruit, lychees and pomegranates. The admission price includes a free banana and a taste of the local banana liqueur. Bananera is open daily from 09:00 to 18:00. Free shuttle buses run from the waterfront.

---

**WATER RESOURCES**

Water is a scarce commodity in Tenerife. Supplies come from rainfall and melting snow on the upper slopes of Mount Teide. Much of the precipitation soaks underground, from where it has to be recovered by making tunnels into the hillsides or digging wells. From these sources the water runs through pipes, which can be seen everywhere festooned across the hillsides to individual farmhouses, which all have their storage tanks. It is a curious fact that all the water supply in Tenerife is in private hands and the release of water is strictly controlled and metered. Demand for water is great, particularly with the growth of the tourist industry, but so far, unlike the eastern islands of the Canaries, Tenerife has resisted the introduction of desalination plants.

## EAST OF PUERTO DE LA CRUZ

On the eastern edge of the Orotava valley is the busy little market town of **Santa Ursula**, in the middle of a wine and banana producing area. It is worth stopping to view its parish church which dates from 1628 and has some fine sculptures and metalwork. Just outside Santa Ursula is the **Mirador de Humboldt**, named after the German explorer who was hugely impressed with this view across the Orotava valley. Further east is the Barranco de Acentejo, with the twin towns of **La Matanza** and **La Victoria**, which gained their names from the final battles between the Guanches and the invading Spanish. La Matanza translates as the 'massacre'. It was here that, in 1494, the Guanches lured the troops of Alonso Fernández de Lugo into an ambush in the Acentejo gorge. The Spanish lost over 900 men, most of them Canarian mercenaries. De Lugo escaped by wearing the blue cape of a foot soldier. He did not give up easily, however, and the following year he was back with a stronger force for a battle just 3km (2 miles) away from La Matanza. This time the Guanches, weakened by disease and in-fighting, were soundly defeated. De Lugo built a church on the site and the town that grew up around it was known as La Victoria (the Victory). Both La Mantanza and La Victoria are agricultural centres and the area still makes pottery in the Guanche style.

---

**HUMBOLDT'S ENTHUSIASM**

The German naturalist and explorer, **Baron Alexander von Humboldt** (1769–1859) came to Tenerife in 1799 with the botanist Aimé Bonpland. It is said that they climbed Mount Teide and visited many other parts of the island. Von Humboldt was most impressed with the **Valle de Orotava** and regarded it as one of the most beautiful parts of the world. Today, the place where he stood is marked by a mirador and there is a plaque which records, in Spanish, his comments on the view.

---

**Opposite:** *Loro Parque, with its wide variety of attractions, has become Tenerife's most visited tourist location.*

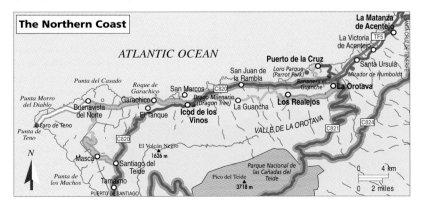

## LA OROTAVA

The coat of arms of La Orotava has the words *villa muy noble y leal* – a most loyal and noble town. Few visitors to its old town would disagree. La Orotava was founded in the 16th century in the prosperous agricultural land of the Orotava Valley. It immediately attracted aristocratic immigrants (their coats of arms can be seen on many of the houses in the older part of the town) and a number of religious orders. The town has some superb examples of Spanish colonial architecture, with richly carved balconies and shady, flower-filled interior courtyards. Add to this some fine churches and convents, plus a few interesting museums and it can be seen why La Orotava makes such an interesting contrast with the coastal resorts.

The **Plaza de la Constitución**, the main square, has sweeping views towards the coast. At the side of the square is the monastery church of **San Agustín**. Dating back to 1694, it is now a music school. Above the plaza is the **Liceo de Taoro**. Built in the 19th century, it was once a school but is now a private club and casino. It is often open to the public for art exhibitions.

Southwest of the main square is the late 19th-century **Ayuntamiento** (Town Hall). The square in front of it and the surrounding streets mark the site of the 'flower carpets', an essential part of the Corpus Christi processions. Behind the Ayuntamiento is the **Hijuela del Botánico**, a beautiful garden which is an offshoot of the more famous botanical gardens in Puerto de la Cruz. It has a collection of over 3000 subtropical plants, including an impressive dragon tree. Check with the tourist office for its irregular opening times.

A short stroll from the town hall is the **Iglesia de Nuestra Señora de la Concepción**, the town's most important church. Distinguished by its twin towers and dome, the church was built in the late 18th century in Baroque style on the site

*Above: Las Casas de los Balcones, a craft centre with a famous embroidery school.*

of an earlier church destroyed by an earthquake. Inside there are statues by José Luján Pérez and Fernando Estévez (a native of La Orotava). Look for the marble altar and tabernacle (both of Italian origin and survivors from the original church) and the superbly carved choir stalls.

Head next to Calle San Francisco, a street that captures the atmosphere of Spanish colonial times. A favourite stop here is **Las Casas de los Balcones** (the Houses of the Balconies). This building is in fact two 17th-century houses which were originally the home of a wealthy local family. They have since been joined together and today house an embroidery school. The exterior has a series of balconies with wrought iron railings. Inside is a charming courtyard with carved wooden balconies festooned with geraniums and ferns. The upper floor is a small museum. The ground floor has a workshop where visitors can watch craftspeople demonstrating pottery, basket making, embroidery and even cigar rolling. Many items are for sale and although prices are high, you can be sure that these are the genuine articles. Las Casas de los Balcones is open Mon–Fri, 09:00–13:30 and 16:00–19:30; Sat 09:00–13:30. There is a small entrance charge to the museum. Opposite is the **Casa del Turista** which dates from 1590 and was once part of a convent. Today it is a craft and gift shop along similar lines to Las Casas de los Balcones, with which it competes. The Casa del Turista has a convenient car park at the rear and its terrace has superb views over the Orotava Valley (open Mon–Fri, 08:30–18:30; Sat 08:30–17:00; Sun 08:30–11:00).

---

**FLOWER CARPETS**

Try to be in La Orotava for the Corpus Christi festival (usually in late May). Scattering flowers on the pavements is not unusual in Spain to celebrate this special festival on the religious calendar, but it has become a fine art in La Orotava. Both flowers and volcanic soil are used for the decorations. The designs are geometric, floral, or depict scenes from the bible. No artificial colouring is used on either the flowers or the soil. The best displays centre on the Town Hall Square and the nearby streets. The first flower carpets in La Oratava date from the 1840s, but the tradition more or less died out until it was revived in 1906 for a visit by King Alfonso XIII.

**Above:** *Iglesia de San Marcos at Icod, one of the most interesting churches on the island.*

---

**STREET NAMES**

Streets in Tenerife are often named after people. Often these will be obscure local doctors or better-known artists, sculptors, scientists or politicians. The names Galdós, Pérez and Morales, for example, are frequently seen. One of the most popular names is **Leon y Castillo**, which originates from two brothers. One was a diplomat and politician, the other an engineer. Both did much to enhance Canarian society.

---

Nearby is **El Pueblo Guanche**, a small ethnographic museum located in a town house which dates back to 1610. There are the usual Guanche artefacts, including a gruesome mummy. There is also a craft shop and a splendid restaurant serving Canarian specialities. At the upper end of Calle San Francisco is the **Hospital de la Santísima Trinidad** (Hospital of the Holy Trinity). It was once a Franciscan monastery before becoming a hospital in 1184. It now cares for the mentally handicapped. Its cloisters are occasionally open to the public – check with the tourist office. Just past the hospital, fork left into Calle Dr González García, popularly known as the **Street of the Mills**. There were once eleven working water mills here grinding cereals for making *gofio*. Only three survive today and they are now powered by electricity.

If time permits visit the **Museo de Artesanía Iberoamericana** in Plaza Santo Domingo. Located in a former monastery, it displays articles from Latin America, including ceramics, musical instruments and textiles. The basement has a collection of Canarian costumes. Open Mon–Fri 09:30–18:00; Sat 09:30–13:00.

## WEST FROM PUERTO DE LA CRUZ

The first town on the road west from Puerto is **Los Realejos**, which has a population of around 30,000. The name means 'royal camp' and the town is divided into two sections, Realejo Alto (Upper Realejo) and Realejo Baja (Lower Realejo). Alto is the oldest of the two settlements and its church, which was built in 1498, is the most ancient in Tenerife. It is here that the defeated Guanche *menceyes* were forcibly baptized. Further west are the attractive agricultural towns of **San Juan de Rambla** and **La Guancha**, which have little to detain the tourist in a hurry.

## ICOD DE LOS VINOS

After 10km (6 miles) the town of **Icod de los Vinos** is reached. As its name suggests, it is in the centre of a wine producing area and its white wine has its own denomination of origin. The wine festival at the end of November can be a riotous affair. The wineries have an open day and it is a custom for youths to hurtle down the steep Calle Calvario on wooden sledge boards. Most people come to Icod to see the 1000-year-old **Dragon tree**, which is over 16m (52ft) high. It is claimed that the Guanche *menceyes* administered justice from beneath its branches. To preserve it the authorities have re-routed a road and supported the trunk with concrete and steel bars.

There is much more to see in Icod. Near the Dragon tree is a shady square with laurels, jacarandas and palms surrounding the 16th-century Church of **San Marcos**. The exterior shows elements of Gothic, Renaissance and Baroque architecture. Do look inside this five-naved church with its *artesonado* ceiling, some fine *retablos* and a huge silver cross from Mexico which is 2m (6ft) high and weighs 47kg (103lb). It is reckoned to be the largest silver filigree cross in the world. A steep lane leads from the church up to the Plaza de la Constitución. It is well worth the climb as the square looks much as it would have done 200 years ago. It is full of fine old trees and surrounded by ancient buildings and bodegas. Another attraction, just a few yards from the Dragon tree, is the **Mariposario del Drago**, a fascinating butterfly park. Here are hundreds of exotic species from all over the world and it is possible to see all the stages of the life cycle, from egg to butterfly. Open daily 09:30–18:00.

In the Plaza de la Constitución, near the Dragon Tree, is the Doll and Puppet Museum. Located in an old Canarian mansion with a charming patio, it displays a range of dolls, puppets and teddy bears. Open daily 09:00–17:00.

### SAN ANDRÉS WINE FESTIVAL

The small town of **Icod de los Vinos** is in the centre of a noted wine producing area and the terraced slopes behind the town are full of vines growing on the rich volcanic soil. The **Festival of San Andrés** on 28, 29 and 30 November celebrates the new harvest and the *bodegas* around the Plaza de la Constitución open their doors for the tasting of the new vintage. The festival concludes with the *bajada de las tablas* when local youths slide down the steep streets on improvised sledges. This tradition is said to date from the times when logs were rolled down to the Bay of San Marcos for the construction of ships.

**Below:** *The Dragon tree at Icod, reputed to be the oldest in Tenerife.*

**Opposite:** *Camel safaris are a popular tourist attraction on Tenerife.*
**Below:** *The Castillo de San Miguel at Garachico, which survived the lava in 1706.*

## GARACHICO

The road westward from Icod gives some superb views down over the coastal town of Garachico, with its distinctive rocky offshore islet, known as the Roque de Garachico. The town was founded by Genoese merchants in 1496 and for many years was the main commercial port of the north coast, exporting wine and sugar to the New World. Disaster struck in 1706 when the nearby Volcán Negro erupted and large parts of Garachico were engulfed in lava, which completely blocked up the port. The town has a long history of misfortune as it has also been afflicted with earthquakes and an outbreak of the plague. However, the town's motto is 'glorious in adversity' and it has continued to thrive, although never regaining its former dominance.

It is well worth strolling around Garachico to take in the sights. An obvious landmark is the **Castillo de San Miguel**, a sturdy fortress which somehow survived the advancing lava. It was built in 1575 to defend the port against pirates. Today, it houses a small collection of rocks, fossils and minerals. Open 10:00–18:00. Head next for the **Plaza Glorieta de San Francisco**, the town's main square. There are a number of notable buildings here. The former **Convent of San Francisco** now functions as the Casa de Cultura and hosts a variety of exhibitions and other events. The old convent also houses the **Museo de las Ciencias Naturales**, which has a fascin-ating account of the 1706 eruption. Take a look at

the convent's church, the **Iglesia de San Francisco**, which has a distinguished *Mudéjar* ceiling. Also in the Plaza is the restored **Palacio de los Condes de la Gomera**, the one-time home of the Counts who also owned the castle. Another square nearby is the **Plaza de Arriba**, where we find Garachico's most important church, the Renaissance-style **Iglesia de Santa Ana**. The original building was mostly destroyed in the volcanic eruption and the present church was rebuilt between 1714 and 1721. It has some fine *retablos* (which is not surprising as Garachico is a religious carving centre) plus some statues by Luján

Pérez. Don't leave the Plaza de Arriba without finding the Statue of Simon Bolivar, who did much in the fight for South American independence from Spain. If you are wondering why Bolivar's statue is in Garachico, it is because his mother was born in the town. Finally, take a stroll around the Parque Puerto de Tierra. In these attractive gardens is the huge 16th-century gateway that once marked the entry to the former port.

The main road now heads southwest towards the pass which leads down to the arid southwest coast. The only settlement of note is **El Tanque**, which is well known for its Camel Centre. Visitors are dressed in Arab clothing and taken on a camel safari, pausing to take mint tea in what is claimed to be a genuine Bedouin tent.

The minor road from Garachico heads west towards the northwestern tip of the island. The land here is known as the **Teno Massif** and it was one of the earliest parts of Tenerife to be formed, probably some 7 million years ago. It is the most inaccessible and most sparsely populated part of the island. To the north of the road from Garachico is the **Montaña de Taco reservoir**, the largest on the island and, unusually, sited in the crater of a volcano. The only settlement of any size is **Buenavista del Norte**. It has a pleasant main square, but has little else of interest except the main church of **Nuestra Señora de los Remedios**, which has a 17th-century painting by Alonso Cano and some ornate *retablos*. Just 11km (7 miles) west of Buenavista is the volcanic headland of **Punta de Teno**, with its distinctive lighthouse and renowned sunsets.

### THE WORLD OF THE BANANA

Tenerife's economy is full of examples of 'boom and bust'. The latest agricultural product to suffer is the banana. It was first used as a cash crop for export in the 1870s, but the trade suffered badly during the Spanish Civil War and later during World War II. While it is still the single most important crop in Tenerife it has strong competition from many Central American republics, where the plantations are run by large American corporations. The Canary Island banana is small and Europeans tend to prefer the larger Central American fruit. In Tenerife, the banana also requires irrigation and many people feel that the precious water would be better used in the more economically productive tourist industry. For an insight into banana growing, visit **Bananera el Guanche** on the eastern outskirts of Puerto de la Cruz.

# The Northern Coast at a Glance

## BEST TIMES TO VISIT

The northern coast is a popular all-year-round destination, but visitors should bear in mind that this is the cloudiest and wettest side of the island, particularly in the winter months. The summer sees rather less cloud and rain and does not experience the high temperatures found in the south of the island. For this reason summer is generally considered to be the best time to visit the area.

## GETTING THERE

The nearest airport is Los Rodeos (Tenerife Norte) just west of Santa Cruz, but most visitors arrive at Reina Sofía Airport (Tenerife Sur) in the east of the island. From here it is a one-hour drive by coach or car to Puerto de la Cruz, using the motorway system. Ferries from the other islands arrive at Santa Cruz and Los Cristianos, from where buses link with Puerto de la Cruz.

## GETTING AROUND

The TITSA bus company runs services from Puerto de la Cruz to other places along the north coast. **Car hire** is cheap and there are numerous hire companies based in Puerto de la Cruz. The motorway system enables drivers to reach all parts of the island quickly, but visitors should be prepared for narrow roads and hairpin bends in the more remote areas – drive carefully.

## WHERE TO STAY

### LUXURY

**Melia Botánico**, Calle Richard J. Yeoward, Puerto de la Cruz, tel: 922 38 14 00, fax: 922 38 15 04. This hotel is situated on the hill above the town close to the botanical gardens. Pool.
**San Felipe**, Avda. de Colón 22, Puerto de la Cruz, tel: 922 38 33 11, fax: 922 37 37 18. Long-established, but modernized hotel with a wide range of facilities and services.
**Tigaiga**, Parque Taoro 28, Puerto de la Cruz, tel: 922 38 35 00, fax: 922 38 40 55. This is a luxury hotel in a hilltop position overlooking Mount Teide and the ocean.
**Semiramis**, Calle Leopoldo Cólogan Zuleata, Puerto de la Cruz, tel: 922 37 32 00, fax: 922 37 31 93. A conveniently placed hotel with good views of the coast. It has its own pool.

### MID-RANGE

**Monopol**, Calle Quintana 15, Puerto de la Cruz, tel: 922 38 46 11, fax: 922 37 03 10. One of Puerto de la Cruz's historic hotels, located in the Plaza de la Iglesia.
**Marquesa**, Calle Quintana 11, Puerto de la Cruz, tel: 922 38 31 51, fax: 922 38 69 50. Monopol's rival neighbour in the same plaza.

**San Telmo**, Calle San Telmo 18, Puerto de la Cruz, tel: 922 38 58 53, fax: 922 38 59 91. A family-run hotel located on the waterfront.
**San Roque**, Calle Estaban de Ponte 32, San Roque, Garachico, tel: 922 13 34 35, fax: 922 13 34 06. Located in an attractive part of the old town.
**Victoria**, Calle Hermano Apolinar 8, La Orotava, tel: 922 33 16 83, fax: 922 32 05 19. A small hotel in a converted and modernized manor house.

### BUDGET

**Los Geranios**, Calle de Lomo 14, Puerto de la Cruz, tel: 922 38 28 10. Comfortable guesthouse.
**Pension la Platanera**, Calle de Blanco 29, Puerto de la Cruz, tel: 922 38 41 57. Small, clean and modern.
**Pension Rosemary**, Calle de San Felipe 14, Puerto de la Cruz, tel: 922 38 32 53. This is a clean establishment, popular among visitors.

## WHERE TO EAT

There is a huge variety of restaurants in Puerto de la Cruz, from elegant international establishments to American fast-food joints and humble tapas bars. It is worth searching out Venezuelan restaurants, run by returning immigrants. Elsewhere in the region Canarian food is the norm.

# The Northern Coast at a Glance

*LUXURY*

**Marquesa**, Calle Quintana, Puerto de la Cruz, tel: 922 38 31 51. Elegant dining on the hotel balcony overlooking the Plaza de la Iglesia.

**Casino Taoro**, Parque Taoro, Puerto de la Cruz, tel: 922 38 05 50. Serves international food with good views over the town.

**Magnolia**, Carretera del Botánico 5, Puerto de la Cruz, tel: 922 38 56 14. Seafood cooked in the Catalan style.

*MID-RANGE*

**Restaurante Cocina Vasca**, Calle de la Hoya 2, Puerto de la Cruz. Cuisine with a Basque flavour.

**Mi Vaca y Yo**, Calle Cruz Verde 3, Puerto de la Cruz, tel: 922 28 52 47. This restaurant serves Canarian cuisine, specializing in shellfish.

**Isla Baja**, Calle Esteban de Ponte, Garachico, tel: 922 83 00 08. Seafront fish restaurant.

**Carmen**, Plaza de la Iglesia, Icod de los Vinos, tel: 922 83 00 08. Canarian food, in a traditional town house.

**Regulo**, Calle Pérez Zamora 16, Puerto de la Cruz, tel: 922 38 45 06. Specialist seafood restaurant.

*BUDGET*

**Il Giardino**, Calle Esteban de Ponte, Garachico, tel: 922 83 02 45. Good food in an old village house.

**Bodega la Muralla**, Calle la Holla 40, Puerto de la Cruz, tel: 922 38 23 01. The tapas here are highly recommended.

**Café de Paris**, San Telmo 10, Puerto de la Cruz, tel: 922 38 40 00. Seafront, French-style café serving excellent breakfasts with croissants.

## TOURS AND EXCURSIONS

Puerto de la Cruz is the main centre for the departure of excursions in the area. The main local theme park is **Loro Parque**, tel: 922 37 38 41, with the world's largest collection of parrots and similar birds, plus dolphins, penguins and a host of other attractions. Another popular excursion is to **Bananera el Guanche**, tel: 922 33 18 53, which illustrates all aspects of banana growing. Many enjoy the **Botanical Gardens** on the southern outskirts of Puerto, while a camel safari at the **Camel Centre** at El Tanque, tel: 922 83 11 91, has its devotees.

**Diving:**
Diving lessons are available at Canarisub, Calle de Esquivel 8, Puerto de la Cruz. Diving is also offered at the Hotel Maritimo, tel: 922 36 28 01.

**Mountain biking:**
Excursions by mountain bike can be arranged, and bikes are also available for private hire. Contact Hotel Tigaiga, Puerto de la Cruz, tel: 922 38 35 00. A number of hiking tours can also be joined at this hotel.

**Covered Wagon Rides:**
Horse-drawn wagon rides through forest land are offered by Cañadas-Trek, tel: 922 10 99 71. The price of the excursion also includes meals.

## USEFUL CONTACTS

There are **Tourist Information Centres** in these towns: **Puerto de la Cruz**, Plaza de la Iglesia, tel: 922 38 60 00. **La Orotava**, Plaza General Franco 1, tel: 922 33 00 50. **Garachico**, Centro de Artesanía el Limonero, Calle Esteban de Ponte 5, tel: 922 13 34 61.

**Disabled Travellers:**
Puerto de la Cruz has a specialist shop for disabled travellers – they hire out wheelchairs and even provide a repair service. Contact Le Ro, Apartamentos Martina, Avenida del Generalisimo, tel: 922 37 33 01.

| LA LAGUNA | J | F | M | A | M | J | J | A | S | O | N | D |
|---|---|---|---|---|---|---|---|---|---|---|---|---|
| AVERAGE TEMP. °F | 53 | 53 | 55 | 57 | 59 | 62 | 66 | 68 | 66 | 64 | 59 | 55 |
| AVERAGE TEMP. °C | 12 | 12 | 13 | 14 | 15 | 17 | 19 | 20 | 19 | 18 | 15 | 13 |
| RAINFALL in | 3.6 | 2.9 | 2.6 | 1.6 | 0.8 | 0.4 | 0.2 | 0.2 | 0.6 | 2.4 | 4.5 | 4.1 |
| RAINFALL mm | 91 | 74 | 66 | 41 | 20 | 10 | 5 | 5 | 15 | 61 | 114 | 104 |

# 5
# The Arid East

Visitors arriving at the **Reina Sofia Airport (Tenerife Sur)** on Tenerife's south coast can scarcely have a worse introduction to the island. The landscape is arid and brown, with the gentle slopes covered with cactus-like euphorbia plants, so that the scenery resembles the coast of nearby Africa. Soulless industrial estates surround the airport interspersed with wind farms to generate electricity. There are numerous patches of *plasticultura* – greenhouses made of plastic in which bananas are grown under irrigation. Fortunately, it is only necessary to go 10–15km (6–9 miles) inland to find that the scenery improves. Steep-sided *barrancos* lead to attractive market towns surrounded by cultivation terraces, roadside wild flowers and extensive forests.

The route southwest from Tenerife's other airport, **Los Rodeos (Tenerife Norte)**, presents a much more attractive picture, with a road leading along the spine of Tenerife, the **Cumbre Dorsal**, making this the most attractive route to the Teide National Park.

There is little development along the east coast, despite the motorway that hugs the shore. An exception is the town of **Candelaria**, the basilica of which contains the image of St Candelaria, which attracts pilgrims from all over the Canary Islands and even further afield. Another small, but developing town is **El Médano**, the nearest resort to the airport and the haunt of wind-surfers. In the extreme south of the area is the **Costa del Silencio**, with small fishing villages such as **Las Galletas** and some of the best golf courses in the archipelago.

### DON'T MISS

**\*\* The Pyramids at Güimar:** ancient pyramids or just a heap of stones?
**\*\* The Basilica and statues at Candelaria:** the Canary Islands prime pilgrimage site.
**\* The Miradors along the Cumbre Dorsal:** giving views to either side of the island and up to Mount Teide.
**\* Wind Surfing at El Médano:** one of the top ten sailboarding locations in the world.

**Opposite:** *The Virgin in the Basilica at Candelaria attracts pilgrims from all over the world.*

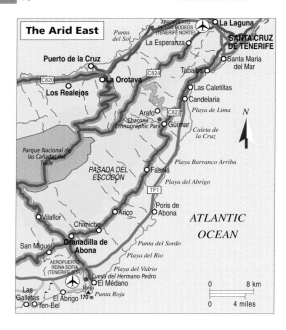

## THE CUMBRE DORSAL

C824 leaves La Laguna and heads up onto the backbone of the island, Cumbre Dorsal, a ridge which runs in a south-westerly direction up to the Teide National Park (described in Chapter 7). The ridge rises from 600m (2000ft) to reach a height of about 2000m (7500ft) and there are numerous miradors along it (*see* panel, this page), giving fine views to both the north and south of the island. The Cumbre Dorsal is in fact a chain of ancient volcanoes that have long since become extinct and also eroded. At the lower levels of the ridge there are a number of scattered hamlets that collectively go under the name of **El Rosario**. The largest settlement in the region is **La Esperanza**, which is well known for its restaurants specializing in country dishes of pork, veal and rabbit. These restaurants are very popular at weekends with the *Santacruceros*. On the higher land around La Esperanza is Tenerife's largest pine forest, which has a number of hiking trails and picnic spots.

## THE EASTERN ROUTES

Drivers travelling along the eastern side of Tenerife have a choice of two routes. For those in a hurry there is the **TF1 Motorway**. For visitors with more time on their hands there is the higher, parallel **C822**, which is considerably slower and includes many dangerous bends. However, it does pass through some attractive scenery and numerous sleepy market towns.

## CUMBRE DORSAL'S MIRADORS

Tenerife's most impressive *miradores*, or viewpoints, are those along the **Cumbre Dorsal**. Leaving La Laguna, the first stop should be at the **Montaña Grande** at 1120m (3675ft), with superb views of Santa Cruz and La Laguna. A little further is the **Mirador Pico de las Flores** at 1310m (4297ft) with even better views in the same direction. Some 7km (4 miles) further is the **Mirador Otuno**, which affords fine views of Mount Teide and north Tenerife. A short diversion from the main road leads to the **Mirador de las Cumbres**, with a vista of the southern half of Tenerife.

## THE INLAND ROUTE

The first town of any importance on the route of the C822 is **Güímar**, the capital of an old Guanche district. The broad Güímar Valley extends seaward and its fertile soil has been terraced for the cultivation of bananas, tomatoes and potatoes. There are also considerable areas of vineyards and Güímar wines have their own DOC. Prominent in the valley is the unmistakable shape of Güímar volcano. The town of Güímar has around 15,000 inhabitants and acts as a market centre for the region. In the main square is the 18th-century church of San Pedro, which is well worth a look. Nearby is the former Convent of San Domingo, which is now the Town Hall. Look for the plaque on a house in the square that marks the birthplace of Isidro Quintero Acosta, who was active in South American politics and introduced the cultivation of cochineal to the Canary Islands. A tortuous road runs northwards from Güímar through the sleepy village of **Arafo** to link up with the Cumbre Dorsal route.

> **CLIMATE**
>
> The east coast of Tenerife is the driest and sunniest part of the island as it lies to the leeward side of the mountains. **Rainfall** is low and mainly confined to winter. **Sunshine** amounts are high, although inland there are often banks of cloud, particularly in winter. The low rainfall results in a semidesert scrub vegetation over much of the coastal plain.

**Below:** *Mirador de Don Martín, one of scores of viewpoints on the island.*

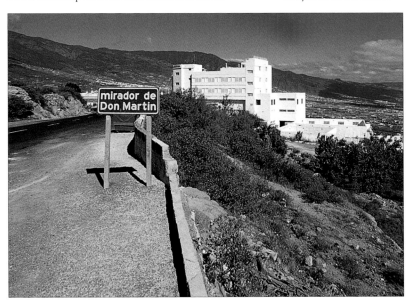

## THE CANARIAN PINE

The most common tree in Tenerife below the sparsely vegetated mountain tops is the **Canarian pine** (*Pinus canariensis*). This is a most useful tree. Firstly, it traps moisture from the wet trade winds, which condenses on the pine needles and falls to the ground, providing a water source for irrigation at lower levels. Secondly, it provides useful timber – the red heart of the trunk is used for building the ornate balconies that are typical of Canarian architecture. In addition, the Canarian Pine is highly resistant to both forest fires and to drought. Little wonder that many areas of Tenerife are being reforested with this important tree.

**Below:** *One of the stone pyramids at Güímar's Ethnographic Park.*

Most people come to Güímar, however, to visit the **Chacona Ethnographic Park**, just north of the town. In the early 1990s, some stone pyramids were excavated here. They caught the attention of Thor Heyerdahl, a Norwegian anthropologist, who was convinced that they were of significance and had similarities with other pyramids in Mexico and Peru. He persuaded his friend, the shipping line owner Fred Olsen, to buy the site and they set up an ethnographical museum here. Recent excavations have turned up a cave that was inhabited by the Guanches and a number of their artefacts have been found, including a basalt sphere. Visitors should be aware, however, that the pyramids are controversial and many authorities consider that they are simply stones that were piled up by local farmers as they cleared their fields for terracing. Whatever the verdict, the site makes a very interesting visit. Apart from the excellent museum there are some reed boats, including the replica of Heyerdahl's reed boat *Ra II*. The museum is open daily, 09:30–18:00.

The next agricultural village is **Fasnia**, which has some interesting stone aqueducts in the vicinity. Fasnia was almost destroyed in 1705 when the local volcano erupted, but luckily the lava stopped just short of the village. Next along is the **Arico** area with the villages of Lomo de Arico, Arico el Viejo and Arico el Nuevo. The only feature to detain tourists here is the village church of San Juan Bautista at Lomo, which has some fine painted panels and an unusual bell tower. A further 15km (9 miles) will bring you to **Granadilla de Abona**, another agricultural centre that markets local tomatoes, potatoes and peppers for tourist centres of the coast. Granadilla has an 18th-century church and a ruined convent that was founded in the 17th century. From Granadilla, the C821 runs northwards in a series of hairpin bends to **Vilaflor** and the Teide National Park. The attractive village of Vilaflor lies at a height of 1400m (4595ft), making it the highest settlement in Tenerife. Its clear air helps people with respiratory problems and the village has become something of a health resort. Vilaflor is well known for its lace making and for the spring water which is bottled nearby and distributed all over the island. Vilaflor is also the starting point for hikes to the so-called **Paisaje Lunar** (Lunar Landscape), which is an area of soft white rock that has been eroded into strange shapes. The final settlement along the inland road is **San Miguel**, which gets its name from the Archangel Michael, the patron saint of the town, whose statue is in the 18th-century church. The town is an important farming centre and traditional pottery has also seen a revival here.

**Above Left:** *Statues of Guanche chiefs line the waterfront at Candelaria.*

## THE COASTAL ROUTE

The Motorway, TF1, follows a route closer to the sea
through the arid coastal plain. The first town of importance is **Candelaria**, a settlement of approximately
11,000 people. It is well known as the main centre of
pilgrimage in the archipelago. The object of all this
adoration is the **Statue of the Virgin of Candelaria**. The
original statue was found on the beach in Guanche times
before being acquired by the Spanish *conquistadores*. The
image was originally kept in a cave, until a sanctuary,
the **Basilica de Nuestra Señora de Candelaria**, was built
in 1526. This was replaced in the 19th century by the
present church and adjacent convent.

The statue, however, is not the original one, as this
was washed out to sea by a tidal wave in 1826. The
present image is in fact a copy of a copy that was
sculpted by Fernanado Estévez. This does not seem to
worry the pilgrims who come from far and wide for the
celebrations on 15 August to pay homage to the Black
Madonna (*see* panel, page 84). There is a large plaza in
front of the church, providing an ideal venue for the
event. On the seaward side of the plaza is a row of nine

imposing bronze statues mounted on plinths of volcanic lava. These represent the Guanche leaders, or *menceyes*, at the time of the Spanish Conquest. The original statues were made of sandstone and were quite badly eroded. If you would like to see these, they can be found on the newly built *rambla* to the north of the town, where they share their environment for the time being with builders' rubble and cranes.

The town of Candelaria itself is pleasant enough, with a very interesting old town and some attractive low-rise apartment blocks on the northern side. Unfortunately, the beach consists of coarse black volcanic sand and there are some dangerous currents, so it cannot really be recommended for swimming.

Tourist developments along this stretch of the coast are few and far between, but one place that looks likely to expand is **Poris de Abona**. At present it is just a small fishing village, but already a holiday resort has been built on the outskirts.

Further south and close to the airport is **El Médano**, which is rapidly becoming a major tourist centre. It has one of the best beaches on the island, but its main drawback is wind. The trade winds are persistently strong here and the beach sand even penetrates hotel bedrooms. This does not bother the windsurfers who swarm to this

**Opposite:** *The Basilica de Nuestra Señora de Candelaria attracts pilgrims from all over the world.*
**Left:** *Farms growing crops under plastic are a common feature of the southeastern parts of Tenerife.*

**Right:** *Web Bar, a popular surfers' internet café on the seafront at El Médano.*

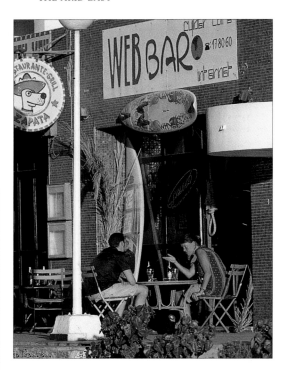

site – they rate it as one of the top ten in the world for this sport. There are windsurfing schools and plenty of shacks where equipment can be hired. El Médano's beaches are divided by the **Montaña Roja**, a striking red-coloured remnant of a volcano, some 170m (550ft) high. The village of El Médano has some quaint, narrow streets with a central square, around which are a number of bars and restaurants. Adjacent to the square is a small sheltered beach that is popular with families. It is worth walking to the west of the village to see the **Cueva del Hermano Pedro**, the cave of the hermit and missionary Brother Pedro. The proximity of the airport and its noisy jets, plus the persistent wind, mean that it is unlikely that El Médano will ever become a major resort like its neighbours to the west.

# The Arid East at a Glance

## BEST TIMES TO VISIT

This is the driest part of the island and sunshine is guaranteed throughout the year, but be prepared for some persistent wind. The inland areas tend to have a layer of cloud that can be slow to clear in the winter. The east coast is certainly an all-year-round destination.

## GETTING THERE

The east coast has the benefit of being the part of the island that is closest to the international airport, so incoming visitors do not have very far to travel. Tourists based in the Puerto de la Cruz area can reach the east coast by service bus or car in under an hour.

## GETTING AROUND

The TITSA bus company runs regular services along the coast road linking the airport with Santa Cruz and the resorts to the west, but the services to the inland towns are less frequent. **Car hire** is undoubtedly the best way of covering the area.

## WHERE TO STAY

Accommodation is thin on the ground along the east coast, particularly inland. Rooms at resorts such as Ten Bel tend to be pre-booked by tour parties. The best bets are at El Médano and Candelaria.

### El Médano

**Playa Sur Tenerife**, Playa del Médano, tel: 922 17 60 13,

fax: 922 17 63 37. Modern hotel set in the dunes and popular with windsurfers.
**El Médano**, Playa del Médano, tel: 922 70 40 00, fax: 922 70 40 00. At the other end of the town on a small headland. Another windsurfers' favourite.
**Hostel Carel**, Avenida de los Principes 22, tel: 922 17 60 66. Cheaper option in town, recently renovated.

### Candelaria

Because of the August pilgrimage, there is a range of accommodation here.
**Gran Hotel Punta del Rey**, Avenida Generalisimo 165, Las Calletillas, Candelaria, tel: 922 50 18 99. Large modern hotel with pool and sea views.
**Tenerife Tour**, Avenida Generalisimo 170, Las Calletillas, Candelaria, tel: 922 50 02 00, fax: 922 50 23 63. Coastal views and pool.
**Campsite**
Tenerife's only official fully equipped campsite is:
**Camping Nauta**, Cañada Blanca, Las Galletas, tel: 922 78 51 18.

## WHERE TO EAT

The inland towns have few possibilities for eating out, but the coastal resorts offer a good choice.

### El Médano

**Avenico**, Calle Chasna 6, tel: 922 17 60 70. One of the best fish restaurants along the east coast.

### Candelaria

**Sobre El Archete**, Calle Lommo de Aroba 2, tel: 922 50 01 15. Imaginative Canarian dishes in a graceful restaurant close to the main plaza.
**Casa Sindo**, Calle Obispo P. Cásares, tel: 922 50 06 09. Typical Canarian cuisine, close to the seafront.

### Los Abrigos

Among the many seafood restaurants in Las Galletas and Los Abrigos, this one stands out:
**La Langostera**, Calle la Marina 18, Los Abrigos, tel: 922 17 03 02. Probably the best of a number of harbourside seafood restaurants.

## TOURS AND EXCURSIONS

Visitors staying in Candelaria will find that it is easy to use public transport to get into **Santa Cruz**. Those staying on the Costa del Silencio will find that there are many organized tours to the **Teide National Park** and the various theme parks to the north of Los Cristianos (these are dealt with in the next chapter). Visitors wishing to see the so-called pyramids at Güimar will need to hire a car.

## USEFUL CONTACTS

The only **Tourist Information Office** in the area is at Reina Sofía Airport, tel: 922 77 30 67, although most of the larger hotels will have a good selection of brochures available.

# 6
# The Southwest

Before the 1960s this part of Tenerife was largely deserted, but then its potential for tourism was realized and development has continued unabated ever since. Although the coastal area has few scenic attractions the region's main advantage is its weather. It can be cloudy, and indeed occasionally wet, inland, but the coastal strip benefits from almost unbroken sunshine throughout the year – an advantage not enjoyed by resorts on the northern coast.

The two main resorts in the southwestern part of the island are **Los Cristianos** and **Playa de las Américas**. The former is based around an old fishing port, but Playa de las Américas was built almost entirely from scratch. The two resorts have now joined up to form a huge tourist conurbation, which is probably the largest on Spanish territory. Apartment blocks and hotels sprawl up the hillsides and sand has been imported to improve the beaches. Clubs, discos and bars abound providing everything for the younger tourist looking for a lively time. A number of **theme parks** have appeared in the surrounding area, which are very popular with families and easily reached on the free shuttle buses. There is also a full range of **water sports** available for the more active visitor.

Development is now moving northwards along the coast, towards the quieter and more up-market resorts of **Puerto de Santiago** and **Los Gigantes**, set against the impressive volcanic cliffs. Further inland, the landscape is arid and uninspiring. An exception is the **Barranco**

**DON'T MISS**

**\*\* Barranco del Infierno:** easy hiking along a stupendous gorge.
**\*\* Las Aguilas del Teide:** best of the theme parks.
**\*\* Los Gigantes:** the towering cliffs of volcanic basalt to the north of Puerto de Santiago.
**\*\* Masca:** remote and picturesque village among great walking country in the Teno Mountains.
**\* Octopus Aquapark:** pools, chutes and slides in this waterpark on the outskirts of Playa de las Américas.

**Opposite:** *The village of Masca among stunning scenery in the northwest.*

**del Infierno**, a deep gorge with a waterfall at the far end. Located at Adeje, just 6km (4 miles) from Playa de las Américas, the *barranco* offers superb walking.

Another popular excursion in the area is to the remote village of **Masca**, set in beautiful mountain scenery in the north of the region. Here outdoor enthusiasts can enjoy a walk down the Masca gorge to the coast. Few visitors to the southwest of the island leave without an excursion to the **Mount Teide National Park**, which is easily reached from the coastal resorts.

## COSTA DEL SILENCIO

The Silent Coast is the name given to the area between Los Cristianos and Reina Sofia Airport. Although this stretch of coastline may once have been quiet, today it is beset with the noise of screeching jets and the throb of music from the bars and discos of a number of modest little resorts. Despite the development, it is not a particularly attractive shoreline. Most of the narrow beaches are of black volcanic shingle interspersed with low cliffs and headlands.

South of the airport, the first settlement reached is the fishing village of **El Abrigo** (shown on some maps as Las Abrigas). So far, it has largely resisted development, but has a handful of cheap seafood restaurants that attract visitors. West of El Abrigo are two of Tenerife's best

### The Southwest

TENO HILLS
Los Llanos
El Volcán Negro 1626 m
LOS FRONTONES
Playa de Juan López
Masca
Santiago del Teide
C820
Punta de los Machos
Tamaimo
Arguayo
Cuevas Negras
Pico Viejo 3105 m
Parque Nacional de las Cañadas del Teide
Los Gigantes
Chío
C823
Puerto de Santiago
Playa de la Arena
Punta de Barbero
Guía de Isora
C821
Punta de Alcalá
Alcalá
Llano Negro
San Juán
Tejina
C821
Playa de San Juán
Vera de Erqués
Callao Gordo
C822
Taucho
N
Punta de Isorana
Trevejos
Callao Salvaje
Armeñime
B. del Infierno
Waterfall
Punta Negra
Adeje
La Caleta
Arona
ATLANTIC OCEAN
Parque Ecológico Las Águilas del Teide
C822
Playa del Bobo
Tenerife Zoo and Monkey Park
Parques Exóticos
Playa de las Américas
Los Cristianos
TF1
El Puerto
Jardines del Atlántico Bananera
0   4 km
Palm-Mar
0   2 miles
Punta de Rasca
Las Galletas
Faro de Rasca

golf courses, namely **Golf del Sur** (tel: 922 70 45 55) and the **Amarilla Golf and Country Club** (tel: 922 73 81 70). The former is generally reckoned to be the most exclusive club on the island, and although it welcomes visitors, they must show proof of their handicap. Golf de Sur has 27 holes, a deep barranco as a major hazard and bunkers of black volcanic sand. Amarilla is an 18-hole golf course and in addition has nine holes of pitch and putt. It also welcomes visiting golfers.

To the west of the two golf courses is the small resort development of **Costa del Silencio**, which gives this stretch of coastline its name. Adjoining Costa del Silencio is the purpose-built resort of **Ten-Bel**. It was constructed by Belgian developers, hence its rather unoriginal name. The two resorts consist of the usual collection of hotels, low-rise apartment blocks and villas separated by subtropical gardens and sports facilities. Because the beaches along this coastline are narrow and shingly, a number of sea-water swimming pools have been developed. Water sports on offer include windsurfing and sailing. A yellow submarine, the Finnish-built *Subtrek*, provides regular trips to see the abundant marine life of the nearby Atlantic sea bed.

The final settlement along the Costa del Silencio is the attractive fishing village of **Las Galletas**. It has benefited from the proximity of Ten-Bel, many of whose visitors make use of the numerous seafood restaurants in the village. Las Galletas now has a small seafront promenade lined with shops and cafés. It is gradually spreading out into the surrounding banana plantations, where you will find *Camping Nauta*, Tenerife's largest camping and caravan site.

**Above:** *Bus services link the resorts with theme parks and other attractions.*

### FERAL EXOTIC BIRDS

Although Tenerife has only a small number of breeding bird species, this is compensated by an interesting exotic blend. Considering the number of theme parks that have large collections of foreign birds, it is inevitable that some of these manage to escape. Some parks, in fact, encourage some of their species to be free-flying. The escapees find that in the benign climate of the Canary Islands they can find plenty of food; many even breed. **Parrots**, **parakeets** and **lovebirds** do particularly well, and flocks of ring-necked parakeets screeching over the apartment blocks are a common sight. Even cage birds such as **zebra finches** (normally resident on the Indian subcontinent) can be seen living in the wild.

**Above:** *The crowded beach between Los Cristianos and Playa de las Américas.*

---

**TIMESHARE TOUTS**

One of the irritations of a holiday in Tenerife is the ubiquitous timeshare tout, who hangs around markets, promenades and other crowded places. Officially known as an 'off property contact', his job is to entice visitors with such ploys as free gifts and holiday offers to go to a location where hard sell techniques are employed. The idea is to persuade visitors to buy a share in a property in which they can take a holiday for one or two weeks a year for life. For some people the idea is attractive, but for many it will be unsuitable. The best advice is not to sign anything until you are absolutely sure of the financial implications and then make sure that there is the usual week's 'cooling off period' during which time you can change your mind.

---

## LOS CRISTIANOS

Popular with package tourists, Los Cristianos was once merely a small fishing port and its boats still supply seafood for much of the southern part of the island. The **harbour** is still the focus of life in the town. The highlight of the day is the arrival and departure of the ferries. Both Fred Olsen and Trasmediterránea run car ferries several times a day between Los Cristianos and San Sebastián on La Gomera (note that tickets are not interchangeable between the two lines). In addition, Fred Olsen operates a high-speed hydrofoil on the route. Some of the ferries go on to the islands of La Palma and El Hierro. The harbour at Los Cristianos buzzes with other water activities. Pleasure boats take visitors to watch whales and dolphins, ocean going yachts wait for good conditions to cross the Atlantic, 'Pirate Ships' take the intrepid along the coast for boozy voyages and a host of other small craft bob at their moorings. Deep-sea fishing excursions can also be booked in the kiosks along the harbour wall and marlin, shark and tuna can be guaranteed. Next to the harbour is a well-kept yellow sand beach, which is lined with chair beds and parasols during the summer months. To the north across the harbour road is the even more impressive **Playa de las Vistas**, with an offshore fountain and a promenade which stretches all the way to Playa de las Américas. Both beaches are lined with cafés, bars and restaurants, many serving excellent seafood. The southern end of the beach is the site of a weekly **flea market**, which attracts tourists by the coachload from many parts of the south of the island. Away from the beach, life revolves around the **Plaza del Carmen**, with its pretty modern church. Leading from the main square are a number of traffic-free alleyways full of attractive shops, many selling duty-free goods and traditional craft specialities. In the suburbs of Los Cristianos, rank upon rank of hotels and apartment blocks stretch up into the surrounding hills. Some of those constructed in the early years of development have all the charm of multistorey car parks, but thankfully those designed more recently have more architectural merit.

## A DAY TRIP TO LA GOMERA

For visitors staying in the south of Tenerife, there is the possibility of taking a day trip to the island of **La Gomera**, which now has a new airport with daily flights from Tenerife Sur to Playa de Santiago. However, many visitors based in the south of the island will still prefer to take the more leisurely ferry. Many local travel agents offer excursions and it is also possible to take a hire car on the ferry and take an independent tour of the island. The voyage to La Gomera (which can be clearly seen from Los Cristianos on most days) takes an hour and a half and there is always the possibility of seeing dolphins and even whales from the boat. If time is at a premium, take Fred Olsen's high-speed hydrofoil, which takes a mere 35 minutes. If the early morning ferry is used, then a stay of eight hours can be enjoyed allowing time to see the best scenic areas on the island. The ferries dock at **San Sebastián de la Gomera**, the main port and capital of the island. This is where Christopher Columbus stopped on his first three voyages across the Atlantic. The object was to take on supplies of water and fresh food, but he also had a romantic interest in a widow, Beatriz de Bobadilla, who was a resident in the town. By the time of his fourth voyage, however, Beatriz had married the formidable Alonso de Lugo, and Columbus wisely took on supplies elsewhere.

La Gomera is one of the smaller Canary Islands,

> ### WHISTLE WHILE YOU WORK
>
> Tourists on organized visits to La Gomera are likey to be treated to a demonstration of *El Silbo*. This 'whistling language' originated in Guanche times when the Gomerans found it easier to communicate across the rugged valleys by whistling rather than shouting. The whistles, achieved with a cupped hand and fingers in the mouth, have a complicated grammar and vocabulary, with over 3000 words identified. It is claimed that a whistled message can be heard over 4km (2½ miles) away. *El Silbo* almost died out, but it has recently been revived and the local children are nowadays obliged to study it at school.

covering about 378km² (146 sq miles). Its landscape is very different from that of Tenerife. There is a frequent cloud cover over the island, so that it is well vegetated, with a dense forest cover in places, and Canary palms common in the lower lying regions. Try to visit the centre of the island, which is the location of the **Parque Nacional de Garajonay** (one of only eight such parks in Spain). The highest point on the island is **Mount Garajonay** in the centre of the park, which rises to 1487m (4878ft). The dense forest cover, however, means that there are few views to enjoy. Garajonay covers some 4000ha (9880 acres) with crags, barrancos and steep slopes. With some 600mm (24in) of rain annually, the park has permanently flowing streams, unlike most of the other Canary Islands. This has resulted in large spreads of cloud forest, including unique remnants of *laurisilva* – dark damp areas dominated by the Canarian laurel (*Laurus canariensis*) and tree heath. The main information centre for Garajonay National Park is at Juego de Bolas, near Las Rosas (open Tues–Sat, 09:30–16:30). As well as information about the Park there is a small garden showing some of the island's main flora. Local crafts such as basketry, pottery and weaving are often demonstrated. The park's information centre is also the start of a number of well-marked walks.

The other scenic feature of La Gomera, not to be missed, is the **Valle Gran Rey** (Valley of the Great King). It was discovered in the 1970s by hippies wanting an alternative lifestyle, putting La Gomera on the tourist map for the first time. Valle Gran Rey is a beautiful steep-sided valley, clothed with terraces growing bananas, papayas and many other subtropical crops.

Don't expect much tourist activity in La Gomera – people come here for the tranquillity! The only resort of any size is **Playa de Santiago** in the

**Below:** *Tourist development on La Gomera is generally low key.*

south of the island. This is the location of the new airport which opened in 2001. The Fred Olsen company have built a hotel complex and there are a few beaches – but don't get too excited, as they are generally narrow and composed of black sand or shingle. Don't look for any volcanic features either. Though the island is largely composed of volcanic rock, there has been no activity for millions of years. If taking a car over to La Gomera, be aware that the roads are narrow and winding. Although the island is small, journeys can take longer than expected.

Tour operators' excursions visit the aforementioned features and the trips usually include a demonstration of the local whistling 'language', which has been handed down from the times of the Guanches (*see* panel, page 91).

## Playa de las Américas

Up until the early 1960s this stretch of coast was a stony, arid area of semidesert, relieved only by a few banana plantations. Then the developers moved in and created an entirely artificial holiday resort. Opinions about Playa de las Américas vary. Its detractors emphasize the noisy nightlife, with clubs, bars, discos and pubs unashamedly designed to appeal to the younger set. With English pubs, German beer gardens and international food, it could be said that you would be hard pushed to know you were actually in Spain. On the other hand, it is a well-planned resort with tree-lined avenues and imaginatively designed apartment blocks and hotels. Most of the hotels in Playa de las Américas have facilities like swimming pools and tennis courts, while their grounds are full of subtropical plants – like miniature botanic gardens. One hotel, the Bahia del Duque, which is in the form of a Canarian village, is probably the most luxurious on the island.

Interspersed with the hotels and apartments are commercial centres. **Centro América**, located near Hotel Las Palmeras, has specialist shops and market stalls. **Santiago III** is a multistorey shopping centre amid an apartment complex of the same name. **City Center**, near La Siesta hotel, has some good specialist shops with duty-free goods. **Shopping Center Bourgainville** also has some

### RENEWABLE ENERGY

Tenerife has no deposits of fossil fuels such as coal, oil or natural gas. Nor can it generate electricity by using running water, owing to low precipitation levels. Inevitably, there has been keen interest in research in renewable forms of energy. Fortunately Tenerife has plenty of sun and wind. It is now standard for new houses and industrial premises to have solar power. Modern wind 'farms' are also appearing in many parts of the island. To see how renewable energy is developing in Tenerife, head for Granadilla in the south of the island where you will find the **Montaña Pelada Technological Park**. Here, an outdoor technological walkway takes you through the latest advances.

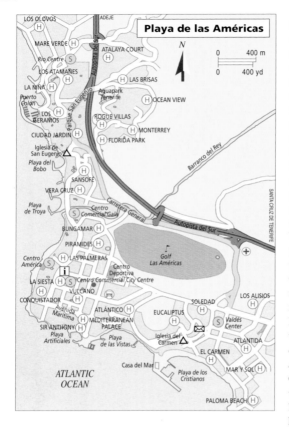

**Playa de las Américas**

high-quality shops. At night, Commercial Centres change their character completely as discos and night clubs open their doors and music throbs, often until daybreak. Playa de las Américas has three small, well-kept **beaches** – Playa del Bobo, Playa de Troya and Playa Colón – with rows of sun beds and parasols; they can get very crowded during the height of the season. Backing the beaches is a tree-lined promenade, and it is now possible to walk to Los Cristianos. Perhaps the most pleasant part of the resort is **Puerto Colón**, a luxurious marina crammed with yachts and backed by chandlers' shops, restaurants and bars. A statue of Columbus points across the sea towards America. Boats and pedaloes can be hired at the marina.

Above all, Playa de las Américas is an all-action resort. In addition to its night life, there is a wide range of activities available, such as go-karting, paragliding, water-skiing, sailing, deep-sea fishing, dolphin watching, windsurfing, diving, jeep safaris and countless others. Make sure that both you and the operators are insured for these adventure activities. Just outside the resort are two of the best golf courses on the island. **Golf Las Américas** (tel: 922 75 20 05) is an 18-hole course designed by John Jacobs close to exit 28 of the motorway. It has a restaurant and driving range. **Golf Costa Adeje** (tel: 922 71 00 00) is near

---

**WATER SPORTS**

The resorts in southwest Tenerife offer all kinds of water sports, ranging from pedaloes, banana boats, parasailing and jet skis to sailing, scuba diving, windsurfing and water-skiing. Swimmers should beware of underwater rocks and strong currents.

the end of the motorway. It has 18 holes with a further nine holes planned. Buggies and clubs can be hired at both courses and visitors are welcomed. A quartet of **theme parks** plus a zoo are within easy reach and free shuttle buses link them with the main hotels. Certainly, no visitor to Playa de las Américas could complain of boredom!

North of Playa de las Américas is the developing resort of Costa Adeje. It is typified by luxury, self-contained hotels with luxuriant gardens, but often isolated from local shops and facilities. The beaches, however, are good.

### THEME PARKS
When the sun and sand pall or the weather is cloudy, visitors (especially those with children) can choose from a number of easily reached theme parks for diversion.

### Parque Ecológico Las Aguilas del Teide (The Eagles of Teide Ecological Park) ★★★
This park opened in 1994 and has proved extremely popular with visitors. Originally it concentrated on displays of free-flying birds of prey, but now there are penguins, dolphins, crocodiles, flamingos and elephants, plus some rides for children – all set in nearly 8ha (20 acres) of beautifully landscaped grounds complete with waterfalls and lakes. The main criticism against the park has been that few of its animals are in fact native to Tenerife, but this does not seem to worry the majority of its visitors intent on a great day out. The park is 3km (2 miles) from Los Cristianos on the Arona road. Leave the motorway at Junction 27. It is open daily 10:00–18:00 (tel: 922 72 90 10) and there is an admission charge.

---

**JEEP SAFARIS**

A good way of exploring the Tenerife countryside is by going on a jeep safari. These four-wheel-drive, off-road vehicles can reach parts of the countryside such as forest trails and rough volcanic terrain which are out of bounds to normal cars. But remember that open-top jeep safaris can be hot, windy and uncomfortable. On these trips, don't expect much in the way of wildlife as Tenerife has few mammals and only a small number of bird species. The scenery, however, will be magnificent and the emphasis will be on having a good time. Choose a reputable company with reliable vehicles.

**Below:** *A meal with a view at a beachside restaurant in Playa de las Américas.*

**Below:** *The local aquapark is popular with children as well as adults.*

## Aquapark Tenerife ★

Also known as Octopus Park, this waterpark makes an excellent alternative to the beaches and will be particularly appreciated by younger visitors. There are numerous pools, water slides, shutes, fountains and simulated waves, all set in attractively landscaped grounds. There is also a large dolphinarium and these aquatic mammals appear in regular shows. The aquapark is located next to the motorway at San Eugenio Alto, Playa de las Américas. Leave the motorway at Junction 29 and follow the signs. Open daily, 10:00–18:00 (tel: 922 71 52 66). Admission charge.

## Parques Exóticos ★★

This site has two main sections, a cactus park and a simulated rain forest. Cacti grow well in the arid landscape of southwestern Tenerife and the gardens display a range of specimens from various parts of the world, some growing to a huge size. The second main attraction is 'Amazonia', a walk-through area of jungle within a huge plastic canopy, complete with humming birds, parrots, iguanas and a host of butterflies. Other parts of the park include a terrapin pool and a wooded area for squirrel monkeys. Parques Exóticos can be reached from the minor road on the east of Los Cristianos or by leaving the motorway at Junction 26. Open 10:00–18:00 (tel: 922 79 54 24). Admission charge.

### Tenerife Zoo and Monkey Park *

The Tenerife Zoo is located right next to the Parques Exóticos, so it is convenient to visit both these places on the same day. The main attractions are the monkeys and other primates, although there are a handful of

**Above:** *A wide variety of cacti can be seen at the Parques Exóticos.*

other mammals to be seen. The main concentration is on animals that appeal to children, such as ponies and parrots. Also associated with the zoo is a firm running **camel safaris**. Visitors are dressed in Arab clothing and taken on a camel caravan safari. The zoo is open daily 09:30–18:00, while the camel caravans run at 30-minute intervals between 10:00 and 18:00 (tel: 922 75 13 68). Admission charge. To reach the Tenerife Zoo, leave the motorway at Junction 26.

### Jardines del Atlántico Bananera **

For those visitors staying in the south of the island this working banana plantation makes a good alternative to travelling all the way to Bananera el Guanche at Puerto de la Cruz. Visits are by guided tours which take place at intervals throughout the day. The first stop is a talk with visual displays about the production of bananas (and other tropical fruit), with a particularly interesting account of how crops in the lowland are irrigated with rain that falls on Mount Teide. The tour then goes into the plastic-covered banana plantations and on to a museum of farming tools and machinery. The gift shop sells banana recipe books, seeds and banana liqueur, while there are, predictably, plenty of banana-based desserts

---

**THE WILD CANARY**

The bright yellow canary trilling in its cage is familiar to everybody and will often be seen in Tenerife. Its wild ancestor, however, is a much different bird. The canary (Serinus canaria) is endemic to Madeira, the Azores and the Canary Islands. In the wild it is quite a drab bird, with striated markings and only a touch of dull yellow-green. It can be seen in a variety of habitats, but usually near pine forests (where it builds its nest) and cultivated fields. Only the male sings and its trilling bears little resemblance to the virtuoso performance of the captive bird.

in the restaurant. Guided tours take place at 10:00, 11:30, 13:00, 15:30 and 16:15 (tel: 922 72 04 03). Leave the motorway at Junction 26 and then follow the signs.

All the theme parks can be reached by free shuttle bus from the main resorts. The brochures in the tourist office show the pick-up places and times. The shuttle buses to Bananera link up with the tour times.

## NORTH FROM PLAYA DE LAS AMÉRICAS

For 20km (12 miles) north of Playa de las Américas the coastline is relatively undeveloped, with only a string of small fishing villages. The most picturesque is **Alcalá** with colourful boats bobbing in its harbour. Away from the sea is an attractive tree-lined square. **Callao Salvaje** and **La Caleta** have little to delay the visitor apart from a few fish restaurants. The only place of any size is **San Juan**, which has a busy fishing fleet, a dry dock and a boat building industry. Watching the morning catch being unloaded is a popular activity. Among the boats operating from San Juan are the ancient sailing boat *Nostramo*, which offers trips to view the cliffs at Los Gigantes, and a launch that runs whale and dolphin watching trips. Inland from these coastal settlements are long stretches of irrigated tomato and banana plantations, while out to sea on a clear day are impressive views of the island of La Gomera.

## PUERTO DE SANTIAGO

Once a small fishing village, Puerto de Santiago is now a growing, up-market tourist resort. The shoreline is mainly rocky, except for the **Playa de la Arena**, a small but clean beach of black volcanic sand. Such is the popularity of Puerto de Santiago that a large sea-shore lido is planned for the near future, along the lines of Lido San Telmo in Santa Cruz. When this scheme materializes,

---

### WHALE WATCHING

The harbour at Los Cristianos is a good place to book a boat trip to watch whales and dolphins. Some of the boats have underwater cameras to watch these magnificent creatures. Whale watching has become so popular that there are now regulations that limit the number of boats taking part in the activity. One of the world's most important colonies of **short-finned pilot whales** (*Ballenas pilotos*) are regularly seen off the southwest coast of Tenerife. They can weigh more than 3000kg (6613lb) and reach up to 5m (16ft) in length. At migration time a number of other species may be seen including **sperm whales** (*Physeter macrocephalus*). Dolphins are relatively common off the waters of Tenerife and include the **common dolphin** (*Delphinus delphis*) and the **bottlenose dolphin** (*Tursiops truncates*). Both are frequently seen swimming and jumping alongside boats.

Puerto de Santiago will become much busier. A few fishing boats still operate from the town, but many of the fishermen make a more profitable living from taking tourists out on boat trips. Behind the beach, tasteful villas, hotels and apartments suggest that this area does not seek to appeal to the mass tourism of the resorts further south. Northwards, Puerto de Santiago merges into its satellite resort of **Los Gigantes** (the giants), another up-market resort, named after the towering cliffs of black volcanic basalt. Reaching over 600m (1970ft) in height, the cliffs stretch for more than 10km (6 miles). Boat trips to see the cliffs run from the Puerto Deportivo (sport harbour) at Los Gigantes. Other boats leave for scuba diving, dolphin watching or game fishing. Some of the boats are glass bottomed. There is a small beach of black volcanic sand nestling against the cliffs that is gently sloping and safe for children.

> **SENIOR CITIZENS IN THE CANARY ISLANDS**
>
> Senior citizens will find that there are many benefits for them on a holiday in the Canary Islands. Many hotels and tour operators offer discounts for long-stay holidays during the winter months, so that the northern winter can be avoided. Pensioners will also find that many concessions are available to them, such as entrance fees to museums, monuments and theme parks. Be prepared, however, to show proof of age.

## INLAND FROM THE COASTAL RESORTS

Inland, there are few places of interest. An exception is the market town of **Adeje**, which has a long history. This was a Guanche regional capital and after the Spanish Conquest it became the power base of the Ponte family, who had originated in Genoa. In the 16th century, they built a fortified residence, the **Casa Fuerte**, which eventually became a centre for the collection of sugar cane produced by slave labour.

It was partly destroyed by fire in the 19th century and was later used as a storehouse for local tomatoes and bananas. There are now plans to turn the Casa Fuerte into a museum. The only other building of interest in Adeje is the **Iglesia de Santa Ursula**, the parish church dating from the 17th century. It has two

**Opposite:** *The cliffs of Los Gigantes reach a height of over 600m (1970ft).*
**Below:** *The market town of Adeje is the starting point for walks along the Barranco del Infierno.*

**DEEP-SEA FISHING**

Visitors wishing to try deep-sea game fishing have plenty of opportunity in the south, where marinas and harbours have boats for hire, including all the necessary equipment for small groups of anglers. The usual fish caught include marlin, swordfish, bonito and tuna. Some boats specialize in shark fishing. Book early to avoid disappointment.

**Opposite:** *Tamaimo is an attractive agricultural village in northwest Tenerife.*
**Below:** *One of the best hikes in Tenerife is along the picture-perfect Barranco del Infierno.*

aisles, a fine coffered ceiling and a Mexican-style bell tower. Inside, you can see a balcony with a wrought iron screen behind which the Ponte family could worship safe from the inquisitive eyes of the local inhabitants. Look, too, for the statue of the *Virgen del Rosario*, attributed to one of Tenerife's best-known sculptors, Fernando Estévez. Most people come to Adeje, however, to hike into the **Barranco del Infierno** – a steep-sided ravine through which a stream runs for much of the year. The 'Valley of Hell' got its name during the Civil War, when it was the site of numerous executions. The Barranco is reached via the road at the side of the Casa Fuerte. This road, incidentally, has a slope steeper than anything likely to be encountered in the ravine. The path that runs through the Barranco is fairly level and crosses and re-crosses the stream several times before reaching a waterfall (which can be quite impressive in the winter). Beneath the waterfall is a plunge pool, which is a welcome swimming opportunity on a hot summer's day. Initially arid, the vegetation becomes more luxuriant as the path proceeds into

the gorge. Look out on the higher slopes for old Guanche caves, where several mummies have been discovered. Allow three hours for the return walk and make sure you have strong footwear. The Bar-Restaurant Otelo, at the entrance to the Barranco, will be difficult to resist at the end of the hike. Those people arriving by car may find parking difficult, so arrive early.

Further north is the market town of **Guía de Isora**. Although recent volcanic lava comes quite close to the town, it is surrounded by fertile soil growing potatoes and tomatoes, while almond blossoms make a stunning sight in the early spring. The parish church of the Virgen de la Luz, is worth a quick visit to see the Artonesado ceiling and the statues by José Luján Pérez.

After the village of **Tamaimo**, the road climbs steeply through hairpin bends to **Santiago del Teide**, which lies in the pass between the Teno Mountains to the west and the Mount Teide volcanic

area to the east. Santiago has a pleasant, wide, tree-lined main street with one or two restaurants and a bodega where you can taste the wines that are grown in the area. The Moorish looking 20th-century church is of interest, with its whitewashed walls and dome. Two minor roads lead away from Santiago del Teide. One leads south to the village of **Arguayo**, close to the lava that dates from the island's last eruption in 1909. There has been a revival in Guanche-style pottery making in the village. The other road leads northwest into the Teno Hills to the pass known as the **Degollada de Cherfe**. From here there are probably the best vistas on the island, with the majestic Teide to the east, the deep valley of the Teno Mountains to the north and away to the west the islands of La Gomera and La Palma. Proceeding over the pass, the road drops down in a series of hairpin bends to the village of **Masca**. Once remote and only accessible by donkey, this pretty village now attracts the tour coaches by the score. An enterprising mayor had the road built, brought water and electricity to the village and set up a small museum (reached via a steep path). The tourist trade does not seem to have ruined Masca, even though a small number of bars, restaurants and gift shops have appeared. The village is also a good centre for hiking. The best walk is down the **Barranco de Masca** to the sea, a distance of around 8km (5 miles) with stupendous views all the way and some varied flora to appreciate. Allow two hours for the walk and arrange for a boat from Los Gigantes to pick you up in order to avoid having to return uphill to Masca.

## SORTING OUT YOUR CAMELS

Many visitors to Tenerife are tempted to try camel riding. As an example, there are opportunities at El Tanque and Los Cristianos Zoo, where riders can be dressed up in Arab clothes for the experience. However, the beast that they will ride is actually a dromedary. The **Bactrian Camel** (*Camelus bactrianus*) has two humps, while the camel which is seen in Tenerife is in fact the **Arabian Camel** (*Camelus dromedaries*) or the **Dromedary**. These are large animals – standing up to 2m (6.5ft) tall – and their colours vary from brown through fawn to almost white. Camels and dromedaries make excellent beasts of burden as they have large storage pockets for water in their stomachs and food reserves in their humps. Tenerife's dromedaries were originally imported from North Africa and today they still have Moroccan handlers.

# The Southwest at a Glance

## BEST TIMES TO VISIT

The sunny climate of the southwest makes it an all-year-round destination. It is particularly popular in winter, however, as it is the nearest area to Northern Europe that has guaranteed warm sun at this time of the year. Expect crowds at all seasons. Wild flowers on the lower slopes of the hills are superb in spring.

## GETTING THERE

The south west of Tenerife is easily reached from Reina Sofía Airport, using the motorway. A trip in a **car** that was hired at the airport, for example, would take approximately 20 minutes to reach Los Cristianos and approximately 50 minutes to reach Los Gigantes. **Taxis** can also be hired at the airport. TITSA **buses** call at the airport en route from Santa Cruz to Los Cristianos and other resorts so they are also available as an option.

## GETTING AROUND

The **motorway**, TF1, runs to the northeast of both Los Cristianos and Playa de las Américas. The other **roads** form a network in the coastal area, but relatively few of the minor roads penetrate any distance inland. **Buses** run by the TITSA company link the main settlements, while free shuttle buses connect the resorts to the theme parks. **Taxis** are cheap and plentiful.

## WHERE TO STAY

There is a vast selection of accommodation available, particularly in the main resorts. Many of the hotels and apartments run to full capacity throughout the year and are pre-booked by tour companies. Visitors who arrive without booking first may find it difficult to obtain accommodation.

### LUXURY
**Hotel Gran Bahia del Duque**, Playa del Duque, Fanabe, tel: 922 74 69 00, fax: 922 74 69 10. Without doubt the most luxurious hotel on Tenerife. Beachside location with pools, subtropical grounds and all facilities.
**Arona Gran Hotel**, Avenida Maritima, Los Cristianos, tel: 922 75 06 78, fax: 922 75 02 43. Modern hotel at the eastern end of Los Cristianos overlooking the beach. Pools, restaurants and fitness centre.
**Mediterranean Palace**, Avenida la Américas, Playa de las Américas, tel: 922 75 75 00, fax: 922 75 75 10. Large hotel with excellent facilities.

### MID-RANGE
**Princesa Dacil**, Calle Penetración, Los Cristianos, tel: 922 75 30 30, fax: 922 79 06 58. A few minutes from harbour; popular with tour groups.
**Los Gigantes**, Calle Flor de Pascua 12, Los Gigantes, tel: 922 10 10 20, fax: 922 86 72 75. Modern hotel with pools and fitness centre.

**Conquistador**, Avenida Rafael Puig 22, Playa de las Américas, tel: 922 75 30 00, fax: 922 79 25 69. Good family facilities.

### BUDGET
**Pension la Paloma**, Corner Calle San Juan and Calle General Franco, tel: 922 79 01 98. Family-run, near harbour.
**Hotel Andreas**, Calle Antigua General Franco, Los Cristianos, tel: 922 79 00 24, fax: 922 79 42 70. Centrally placed commercial hotel.
**Pension Corisa**, Edificio Andreas, Los Cristianos, tel: 922 79 07 92. A basic but conveniently located pension.

### La Gomera
Visitors on an excursion to La Gomera might want to stay longer – fortunately there is plenty of accommodation.

### LUXURY
**Parador de San Sebastián de Gomera**, Balcón de la Villa y Puerto, tel: 922 87 11 00, fax: 922 87 11 16. Set in a colonial-style mansion; one of the best paradors in the chain.

### MID-RANGE
**Garajonay**, Ruiz de Padrón 17, San Sebastián, tel/fax: 922 87 05 50. A convenient base for touring, but has no restaurant.

### BUDGET
**Pension Las Vueltas**, Playa La Claera, tel: 922 80 52 16. Cheap option for touring the Valle de Gran Rey area.

# The Southwest at a Glance

## Where to Eat

Visitors to the main resorts are swamped with choice when it comes to restaurants, from simple Canarian food to international menus and exotic far eastern establishments. There are prices to suit all pockets.

### LUXURY

**Casa Pancho**, Playa de la Arena, Puerto de Santiago, tel: 922 10 13 23. Original food on terrace overlooking the beach.

**Hotel Jardín Tropical**, Promenade, Playa de las Américas, tel: 922 75 01 00. The hotel has two excellent prizewinning restaurants open to non-residents: **El Patio** and **Las Rocas**.

### MID-RANGE

**Otelo**, Barranco del Infierno, Adeje, tel: 922 78 03 74. A popular Canarian restaurant situated at the entrance to the gorge. It serves good rabbit dishes.

**Doña Juana**, Playa Azul, Playa de las Américas, tel: 922 79 66 53. Excellent Canarian cuisine, specializing in seafood.

**Casa del Mar**, Esplanada del Muelle, Los Cristianos, tel: 922 79 32 75. This award-winning seafood restaurant is situated close to the harbour.

**El Pescador de Alcalá**, Alcalá harbour, tel: 922 86 50 80. Large and popular seafood restaurant in this small fishing village.

### BUDGET

**Pailebot**, Promenade, Los Cristianos. Cheap Canarian food with friendly service. There are a number of reasonably priced Indian and Chinese restaurants in the main resorts. Try **Gandhi**, Calle Juan Reverón Sierra, Los Cristianos, tel: 922 75 16 32, with its comprehensive Indian menu. There are also a host of cheap pizzerias, many with take-away services. Tapas bars are few and far between, but a good exception is **El Cine**, Calle Juan Boriajo 8, Los Cristianos.

### La Gomera

**Casa del Mar**, Avda. Fred Olsen 2, San Sebastián de la Gomera, tel: 922 87 12 19. Close to the harbour, this popular restaurant attracts both locals and tourists.

## Tours and Excursions

**Boat trips** are popular from Los Cristianos for whale and dolphin watching. Boats also leave from Los Gigantes to view the cliffs. A day trip by ferry to **La Gomera** is another possibility. There are a number of **theme parks** close to the main resorts,

mainly served by free shuttle buses. **Jeep safaris** can be booked at most hotel desks. The most popular excursion is to the **Mount Teide National Park** to see the wide range of volcanic features and to take the cable car to the summit.

## Useful Contacts

There are **Tourist Information Offices** at:
**Los Cristianos** – Centro Cultural, Avda. Penetración, tel: 922 75 24 92. Open Mon–Fri, 09:00–13:00.
**Playa de Las Américas** – Urb. Torvisas, opposite Hotel La Pinta, tel: 922 75 03 66. Open daily, 09:00–16:00.
**Ferries:**
Los Cristianos is the ferry port for the three western islands of La Gomera, El Hierro and La Palma.
**Lineas Fred Olsen**, tel: 922 79 02 15, runs ferries to San Sebastián de Gomera and one boat a day goes on to Santa Cruz de la Palma.
**Trasmediterránea**, tel: 922 28 78 50, operate ferries and hydrofoils to San Sebastián de la Gomera and a daily boat to El Hierro. Two ferries a week travel to La Palma.

| REINA SOFIA | J | F | M | A | M | J | J | A | S | O | N | D |
|---|---|---|---|---|---|---|---|---|---|---|---|---|
| AVERAGE TEMP. °F | 65.1 | 64.7 | 66.7 | 66.7 | 68.3 | 71.6 | 75.2 | 76.6 | 76.6 | 74.5 | 70.7 | 67.1 |
| AVERAGE TEMP. °C | 18.4 | 18.2 | 19.3 | 19.3 | 20.2 | 22 | 24 | 24.8 | 24.8 | 23.6 | 21.5 | 19.5 |
| HOURS OF SUN DAILY | 6.1 | 6.6 | 6.8 | 6.5 | 7.5 | 7.6 | 8.4 | 8 | 6.2 | 6.5 | 5.7 | 6.2 |
| RAINFALL in | 0.3 | 0.72 | 0.55 | 0.26 | 0.79 | 0 | 0 | 0 | 0.51 | 0.48 | 1.81 | 0.61 |
| RAINFALL mm | 7.7 | 18.3 | 14.2 | 6.5 | 2 | 0 | 0.2 | 0 | 1.3 | 12.2 | 46 | 17.3 |

# 7
# Mount Teide National Park

If the visitor to Tenerife has only enough time to make one excursion, it should certainly be to the Mount Teide National Park (or, to be strictly correct, Las Cañadas del Teide National Park). Mount Teide itself dominates the island. At 3718m (12,198ft) it is the highest point on the Canary Islands and indeed the tallest mountain in all of Spain. Its perfect cone shape makes clear its volcanic origins and although it is at present dormant, there are many well-preserved volcanic features to the south of the main peak in the area known as Las Cañadas. (The word *Cañadas* derives from the gravelly plains beneath the main peak.) Las Cañadas del Teide National Park was set up in 1954 and covers an area of 13,571ha (33,534 acres), making it the fifth largest reserve in Spain. The entire park lies at 2000m (6561ft) above sea level.

One of the first recorded ascents of Mount Teide was by the German scientist Alexander von Humboldt in 1799. Today, over 300,000 people climb to the summit annually. The amazing moonlike landscape of Mount Teide and the wonderfully clear air around its summit has led to it becoming a popular location for filming. Films shot here include *The Planet of the Apes* and *The Ten Commandments*. Apart from its volcanic features, the park has a wide range of unusual flowers, plus a small number of rare bird species.

Mount Teide is one of nine national parks in Spain. Three of these are in the Canary Islands – Mount Teide on Tenerife, the Timanfaya National Park ('Mountains of

## DON'T MISS

**\*\*\* Cable Car to the top of Mount Teide:** for superb views of volcanic features, the rest of Tenerife and many of the other Canary Islands.
**\*\* The Roques de García:** fantastic rock shapes in the centre of the National Park.
**\*\* Parador Nacional de las Cañadas:** stay the night at this state-run hotel and watch the sun rise and set on snow-capped Mount Teide.
**\*\* Las Cañadas Caldera:** enjoy the lunar landscape of this huge collapsed crater.

**Opposite:** *The cable car transports visitors close to the summit of Mount Teide.*

### OBSERVATORIES

The **Izana Astronomical Observatory**, with its white towers and domes, is run by the university at La Laguna, but scientists from several nations share the facilities. There is another observatory at Roque de los Muchachos on **La Palma**. The sites were chosen for clarity of the air on the Canary Islands. The Tenerife observatory special-izes in the study of the sun, while the one on La Palma concentrates on the night sky.

**Opposite:** *A number of the miradors en route to Mount Teide offer quite spectacular views.*

Fire') on Lanzarote, and the Garajonay National Park, a cloud forest reserve, on the island of La Gomera. National parks form the highest level of conservation in Spain, closely followed by natural (or nature) parks, such as the Corralejo Dunes on the island of Fuerteventura.

## ROUTES TO TEIDE

There are four main routes leading to Mount Teide National Park and there is much discussion among visitors and tourists alike as to which of these routes ranks highest in terms of scenery. It would probably be advisable to choose the nearest route from the resort where you are staying in order to get there early in the morning before the crowds, and then return by a differ-ent route later in the day.

Visitors who are staying in Puerto de la Cruz should preferably take the C821 via La Orotava. The winding road has several miradors giving views northwards over the Orotava Valley. At one of these, the **Rosa de**

**Piedra**, there is a rock face with a gigantic structure resembling a stone rose. There is also a trout farm at Aguamansa and you will pass a stretch of pine forest before reaching the visitors' centre and the national park boundary at El Portillo.

The second route, and the longest, runs from Santa Cruz and La Laguna along the ridge of the Cumbre Dorsal. Around Esperanza the landscape is mainly farmland and then the route passes through a long stretch of Canarian pines. Look out for the monument which marks the spot where General Franco had an alfresco lunch (believed to be a paella) with some of his army supporters just a fortnight before the outbreak of the Spanish Civil War. There are also a number of miradors on this route giving vistas over both the north and south coasts. Don't miss the **tarta** – a strange strata of volcanic ash that looks like layers of a cake. Further along, on the south side of the road, are the white towers of the **Astronomical Observatory** run by the Department of Astrophysics at La Laguna University (*see* panel, this page) This route joins the Puerto de la Cruz road at El Portillo.

Visitors staying at the main resorts of Los Cristianos and Playa de las Américas in the southwest of the island have a choice of two routes. The most tortuous road

### LAVA TYPES

Mount Teide and the surrounding area exhibit many types of volcanic material, both liquid and solid. When molten **magma** erupts from a volcano, the eventual form of the lava depends on a number of factors, including its chemical composition and the rate of cooling. The descriptive names that are given are often Hawaiian in origin, for it was in these islands that the first research was carried out. **Aa** (pronounced 'ah-ah') lava is viscous material that cools slowly and has a dark, clinker-like appearance. **Pahoehoe** (pronounced perhoyhoy) lava is glassier and lighter in colour and often cools as ropey lava. Some lava cools in the form of **pillows**, probably after contact with water. **Basalt** is a fluid black lava that travels for long distances and cools in hexagonal columns. It is the most common volcanic rock on Tenerife.

leaves the coast near El Médano and climbs up through Granadilla de Abona and Vilaflor with hairpin bends flanked by vineyards and terraces growing tomatoes and other crops. It is worth stopping at the Mirador San Roque where there are superb views across the terraced hillsides towards the island of La Gomera. Just past Vilaflor, a hiking track leads to the **Paisaje Lunar** or Lunar Landscape – an area of white volcanic ash that has been eroded into pointed columns and other strange shapes. The road continues through pine forests to reach the western end of the national park at Boca de Tauce.

Visitors staying in the more northerly resorts of Los Gigantes and Puerto de Santiago should take the route via Tamaimo and Chío, the road taken by most of the tour coaches. There are spectacular views westward to the islands of La Palma and La Gomera, before the road passes through an expanse of pine forest. The picnic sites here are good spots to see the rare blue chaffinch. On the left-hand side of the road are large stretches of black lava, which date from the eruptions of 1798 and still look very fresh. Shortly afterwards you reach Boca de Tauce, the entrance to the national park. Visitors using public transport should take bus 348 from Puerto de la Cruz.

## THE WEATHER ON MOUNT TEIDE

It obviously makes perfect sense to visit Mount Teide National Park on a clear day, but Mount Teide is so high that it is frequently above the layer of cloud that forms between approximately 500m (1640ft) and 1500m (4920ft). It is possible that you might emerge from the dense cloud cover into bright sunshine when entering the park. The peak of Mount Teide is often covered in snow during winter, but even at this time of year it is quite possible to get rather badly burnt by the sun in the clear air. Chilly winds at this height are very common, and it is therefore advisable to bring warm clothing whatever the season. Humidity is very low, nearly always below 50 per cent.

## GEOLOGICAL HISTORY OF MOUNT TEIDE

The Canary Islands were formed when magma forced its way through the earth's crust creating volcanoes and islands. The earliest of the Canary Islands to be formed in this way were Fuerteventura and Lanzarote in the east. These islands, because of erosion, are low-lying. The most recently formed volcanic islands are in the west and include Tenerife.

**Opposite:** *The distinctive white towers and domes of the Izana Astronomical Observatory, located to the east of Mount Teide.*
**Below:** *The road through the national park gives excellent views of the area's volcanic features.*

There have been numerous volcanic episodes in Tenerife's volcanic history, which probably began between 8 and 12 million years ago. Mount Teide is just the latest in a series of volcanoes to erupt on the island. One of its predecessors is thought to have been nearly 5000m (16,400ft) in height and of a type known as a shield volcano. Its peak eventually collapsed forming a megacrater or **caldera**. This is the giant amphitheatre known today as Las Cañadas. The walls of the caldera are in places 16km (9.5 miles) apart and the circumference measures 45km (28 miles). Mount Teide has formed within the caldera on its northern edge partly burying the crater wall.

Mount Teide probably started forming around 600,000 years ago. In historical time, Columbus noted that the volcano was smoking when he sailed past on his way to the New World in 1492. There were certainly three eruptions in the 18th century, with a major flow of lava occurring in 1798. The so-called *Las Narices del Teide* (Teide's nostrils), a series of small craters on the mountain's southwestern flank, date from this time. A minor eruption in 1909 was the last significant volcanic event. Teide is dormant at present, but experts suggest that the volcano is far from extinct.

**Opposite:** *One of the graphic displays at Mount Teide National Park's visitors' centre.*
**Right:** *The peak of Mount Teide with Los Roques in the foreground.*

## THE FEATURES OF THE NATIONAL PARK

Visitors entering the national park from the resorts in the west will arrive at **Boca de Tauce**, where there is a notice board showing a diagram of the view towards Mount Teide. The different types of lava flow can be clearly seen here, while to the right is the first of the *cañadas*, the **Llano de Ucanca**, which may mark the bed of an old crater lake.

### Centro de Visitantes ★★

In many ways, however, it is better to enter the park from the east, because where the roads from La Orotava and La Laguna meet, at El Portillo, is the **Centro de Visitantes**. The visitors' centre is open 09:00–16:00 and it is well worth spending some time looking at the numerous displays and models to get your bearings and locate the main features of the park.

The centre is accessed through a mock-up of a lava tube (a cave which is formed within moving lava) complete with the roars of volcanic eruptions. There is an audio room here, which provides a short video

### A CHILD-FRIENDLY ISLAND

Do not worry about taking babies or young children to Tenerife, as they will be made very welcome. Spanish children keep late nights and are not excluded from any family activities. Waiters traditionally make a huge fuss of small children who come to their restaurants and will prepare special portions for them. Older children will find plenty to occupy them from sandy beaches to theme parks and boat trips.

### COLOURFUL VOLCANIC ROCKS

Visitors to the Mount Teide National Park are often fascinated by the variety of colours in the volcanic rocks, particularly in the area known as Los Azulejos, which is named after the brightly coloured Spanish tiles. Generally speaking volcanic material becomes lighter in colour with age. Many of the darker lavas are full of **obsidian**, a black glassy mineral that has cooled quickly before crystal structures have had time to form. The lighter coloured gravelly materials are usually composed of **pumice**. Other rocks owe their colours to their **mineral content**, iron staining the rocks brown and red, while copper produces green and blue tints.

programme that is shown at regular intervals in a variety of languages, dealing with the national parks of the Canary Islands in general and Mount Teide in particular. There is also a bookshop where you can buy brochures and other publications outlining the park's flora and fauna. The visitors' centre can also provide useful information about the numerous walking trails within the park – it is essential to call here before walking in the winter months as some of the routes may be closed in bad weather. You can either walk independently or join one of the guided walking tours organized by the centre.

Make sure you visit the 'garden' at the back of the centre, where paths meander around beds full of flowers and shrubs typical of the park. Clustered about the visitors' centre there are also several restaurants, which provide an excellent opportunity for a lunch stop.

The road from El Portillo runs westwards through the heart of the national park. To the left are three volcanic peaks – **Las Mostazas**, **Montaña Rajada** and **Montaña Blanca**. The latter is the starting point for a number of treks to the top of Mount Teide. All around the area here are wide stretches of yellow and red volcanic ash, interspersed with the occasional layer of black obsidian, which the Guanches used as a cutting tool. To the left of the road is the area known as **Arenas Blancas** (which means 'White Sands'), with its dunes of gravelly pumice resembling a desert.

### Cable Car ★★★

Shortly, on the right-hand (north) side of the road, is the **Cable Car Station**. Two small gondolas operate at a time, taking only eight minutes to transport visitors to **La Rambleta**, which is just 170m (557ft) below the summit of Mount Teide. To walk the last 170m to the summit requires a permit, obtainable from the National Park office. Permits are limited to 150 per day, and applicants will need to show their passports. The crater itself is very dangerous and out of bounds to visitors.

There are two additional signposted paths – one goes westward past a number of fumeroles belching sulphurous smoke and gives a good view of **Pico Viejo**, at a height of 3105m (10,187ft), as well as its impressive crater which is approximately 800m (2624ft) in diameter. The other path runs in an easterly direction to a mirador passing some superb tongues of lava en route.

**Opposite:** *Layers of pumice, ash and lava exposed at the roadside.*
**Below:** *Views from the upper station of the cable car are the best in the Canary Islands.*

Be prepared to stand in a long queue in order to board the cable car – a two-hour wait is not unusual, so come early in the morning. The cable car runs from 09:00–16:00, with the last car leaving the top station at 17:00. Note that the cable car may not run in icy or windy conditions. There is a bar-restaurant at the lower cable car station that is open from 09:00–17:00.

Visitors should also be aware that the car park at the cable car station can become seriously overcrowded – another good reason to arrive early.

### Parador Nacional de las Cañadas *

The road now crosses a low pass, the **Puerto de las Cañadas** at a height of 2300m (7545ft), dropping down southwards until the **Parador Nacional de las Cañadas** appears on the left. This is the only accommodation within the park boundaries and makes an excellent base for a few days' walking. It has a restaurant and shop that are open to the public and alongside there is a small Tourist Information Centre, with displays and literature on the geology and wildlife of the park. Note

**Below:** *The easy ramble around Los Roques is the most popular walk in the national park.*

**Left:** *The Roques de García may be part of a volcanic dyke or the remains of an old crater wall.*

that the area around the Parador can become crowded with coach parties. Nearby is a small hermitage, the **Ermita de las Nieves**.

Visitors should note that the parador is very popular and is often fully booked. To ensure accommodation and avoid disappointment, it would be best to book ahead (tel/fax: 922 38 64 15). It is well worth the effort – watching the sun rise and set on the snow-capped peak of Mount Teide is one of the most evocative experiences you can have in the Canary Islands.

### Roques de García ★★

Almost opposite the hermitage are the most photo-graphed features of the park, the **Roques de García**, a series of strangely eroded volcanic rocks. The origin of the rocks is debatable. One suggestion is that they are part of an old crater wall, while another, more plausible theory is that they are part of a dyke or layer of hard intrusive igneous rock.

The most impressive of the rocks is the **Roque Chinchado**, which rises to a height of 30m (98ft) from a narrow base. This startling shape features on Spain's 1000 pesetas note.

From the Roques de García there is a fine view over the **Llano de Ucanca**, the most westerly of the *cañadas*. Look for the rocks known as **Los Azulejos** – they are

**IDENTIFYING YOUR POLICEMEN**

Hopefully, visitors to Tenerife will not need to contact a policeman – which is just as well, because, confusingly, there are three different police forces operating in Spain. Firstly, there are the **Policía Municipal**, who wear blue uniforms and carry out minor duties such as parking and traffic control. Secondly, there are the **Policía Nacional**, who have brown uniforms, and it is to this group that you should go if you are robbed or burgled. Finally, there are the **Guardia Civil**, who wear light green uniforms and who in the past were easily identified by their shiny black hats. Once greatly feared, the Guardia Civil have a less important role in modern democratic Spain. All Spanish police are armed and not noted for their sense of humour. It is not a good idea to adopt a frivolous approach towards them!

**Above:** *Hiking on one of the lower forest paths near Mount Teide.*

stained jade green by the iron and copper in the strata. Another strange rock formation here is the **Zapato de la Reina** (the Queen's Shoe), which resembles a high-heeled shoe. The road through the park finally reaches the western end at **Boca de Tauce**.

Be prepared for crowds at the Roques del García. This is a regular stop for the tourist coaches and there can be hundreds of people swarming along the paths (which are becoming seriously eroded in places) and on the viewing terraces. Late afternoon, when the tourist coaches have gone, is probably the best time to appreciate the magnificence of the Roques.

### CLIMBING MOUNT TEIDE

From the main road through the national park a climb to the top of Mount Teide looks easy enough, but this is deceptive and it should only be attempted by serious and well-equipped hikers. The usual route to the summit starts from a car park situated on the main road approximately 2km (1.25 miles) east of the cable car station. The track is well defined, but because of the loose nature of the surface material and the thin air at this altitude, the hike can be exhausting.

The route heads first for **Montaña Blanca** – named after the white pumice lying around there – and then proceeds upwards in a series of broad curves. Look out for **Los Huevos del Teide** (the Eggs of Teide), which are huge, rounded, black volcanic rocks.

At a height of around 3260m (10,695ft) the track reaches the **Altavista mountain hut**. Many climbers spend the night at this refuge in order to be able to see the sunrise from the peak, which can be quite a magical experience. The hut is open in the summer months only between 17:00 and 10:00. You can book a place in this shelter (tel: 922 23 98 11). Uphill from the hut it is worth making a diversion to the **Cueva del Hielo** (the Ice Cave), which is festooned with icicles throughout the year.

Once you have returned to the main path, a further 20 minutes' walk brings you to **La Rambleta**, where the upper cable car station is located. From here it takes another 20 minutes up the **Pan de Azúcar** (Sugar Loaf) to reach the crater rim, passing along the way some smoking fumeroles, where for the greater part of the year it is comforting to warm your hands in the hot vapours. The summit is usually in full sunlight even though it may be cloudy further below. The views can be stupendous and from here you can pick out the islands of Gran Canaria, El Hierro, La Gomera and La Palma, as well as large parts of Tenerife. The total climb is around 1500m (4920ft) and should take between three and four hours.

**Some words of warning**: Don't think of attempting the climb in inclement weather; don't ever climb alone; make sure that you are well equipped; check the prevailing weather conditions at the El Portillo visitors' centre; and always remember that oxygen is in short supply on the summit, so forget the whole idea if you have respiratory problems.

Visitors who are physically fit but who are inexperienced in mountain walking are strongly advised to join a guided group organized by the National Park staff. Book well in advance by calling ICONA (tel: 922 29 01 29). Alternatively, it is possible to book at their office at Calle del Pilar 1, Santa Cruz.

---

**SAND FAR FROM THE BEACH**

Visitors are often surprised to see large areas of sand in the Mount Teide National Park. This phenomenon has been caused by **weathering**. Low temperatures at night, when the numbers drop down to below freezing point, are contrasted with very high temperatures during the day, when readings often rise to above 38°C (100°F) on the south-facing slopes. This causes stress in the rocks, causing them to break down into granules in their constituent mineral parts. This process is called **mechanical weathering**. The best place in the Mount Teide National Park to see a large expanse of weathered sand is in the area known as Arenas Blanca ('White Sand'), which is located just to the south of the main road going through the park. Here, the wind has actually blown the weathered material into dunes that give the impression of a mini-Sahara.

## OTHER WALKS IN THE PARK

The visitors' centre offers a total of nine guided walks varying in degrees of difficulty and lasting between 30 minutes and six hours. It is essential to book these guided walks in advance by telephoning ICONA (tel: 922 29 01 29). In addition, there is a network of 21 walking trails that can be used by walkers independently, six of which are signposted and have stopping points with information boards.

There is one special route that has been designed with **handicapped** people in mind. Walkers should remember that they are not allowed to stray from the marked trails.

### Information Boards

Possibly the most impressive aspect of a visit to the Mount Teide National Park are the numerous information boards that appear in a variety of places. The boards usually have a labelled sketch that mirrors the view in front of the observer. The scenery is then described and explained in both Spanish and English, so that the visitor without even a basic knowledge of

**Left:** *One of the many information boards that offer visitors a description of the park's scenery.*
**Opposite:** *A mobile shop touts for business at a viewpoint just outside the national park.*

geology can appreciate and understand the scenery. It is easy, for example, to distinguish between acid and basic lavas, to make an educated guess at the varying age of the lavas depending on the amount of vegetation that has begun to grow on their surfaces, and to differentiate between a dyke and a sill. The information board at the western end of the national park near Boca de Tauce is particularly helpful.

## THE WILDLIFE OF LAS CAÑADAS DEL TEIDE
### Fauna

Mammals are shy and elusive in the park and only **rabbits** are likely to be seen. **Mouflon** were introduced to the park in 1971, but research has shown that they have a detrimental effect on the native plants, so their numbers are now being culled. As a result they are extremely shy and very cautious. **Bats** can be seen at dusk and the occasional Canarian **lizard** may be observed basking on a rock.

There are plenty of birds in evidence. The most common bird is the small, brown and unobtrusive **Berthalot's pipit**, which can often be seen in small groups around the parador. Look skyward for **plain**

---

### THE GIANT BUGLOSS

Mount Teide National Park is noted for its remarkable flora, with a number of species which are endemic not only to Tenerife, but to the park itself. Pride of place goes to the **giant bugloss** (*Echium wildpretii*) known in Spanish as the *Tajinaste rojo*, with tall red flower spikes that can reach up to 2m (6.5ft) in height. It flowers in May, but later in the year the dead flower heads can look equally attractive. The rare **Teide violet** (*Viola cheirathifolia*) was discovered by Humboldt in the 19th century. It can be seen on the highest parts of the park, where it flowers after the snows have melted. One of the most abundant plants in the park is the **Teide broom** (*Spartocytisus supranubius*), a hemispherical shaped bush with aromatic pink and white flowers blooming in late spring and early summer.

At 3718m (12,198ft), the **Pico del Teide** is Spain's highest mountain. Nearby peaks include **Pico Viejo** at 3105m (10,187ft) and **Montaña Blanca**, reaching 2750m (9023ft). These can be compared with the highest peak on mainland Spain – **Mulhacen** in the Sierra Nevada range, rising to 3482m (11,423ft). Snow can occur on the top of Mount Teide in winter, but on Mulhacen, because of its higher latitude, snow remains throughout the year, supporting an important skiing industry.

swifts and buzzards, while **great grey shrikes** are often seen, sitting on telephone wires and other prominent perches. At lower levels, especially at the forest picnic sites, the **blue chaffinch**, indigenous to Tenerife, can be very tame. **Butterflies** can be common, particularly during the spring, with the **Canary blue** and the **monarch** most likely to be fluttering past.

## Flora

Despite the great height and the aridity of the landscape, a surprising range of wild flowers proliferates in the park, including 45 endemic species. The star of the show is the enormous **giant bugloss** (*Echium wildpretii* or *Tajinaste rojo*), which has a red floral spike that can be around 2m (6.5ft) in length. Other endemics include the **Teide violet**, which was discovered by von Humboldt, the **Teide daisy** and the **Teide broom**.

Remember that it is forbidden to collect rocks, plants and animals. It is also prohibited to light fires, camp overnight and use any roads or tracks that are not open to the public. Needless to say, it is against regulations to leave litter in the park.

**Below:** *The only vegetation that survives in the national park must be able to cope with the arid climate and an acid soil.*

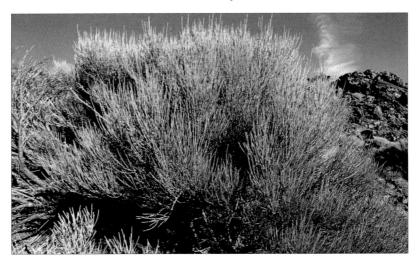

# Mount Teide National Park at a Glance

## BEST TIMES TO VISIT

The park can be spectacular in **winter**, when there is often deep snow, but this can lead to problems of access, as footpaths may be closed, roads blocked and the cable car may not be running. In the **summer** the park may be crowded and there may be long delays on the cable car. **Spring** is probably the best time to visit, with the wild flowers at their best and a capping of snow on the higher parts of the mountain. Whatever time you visit, come early and, if possible, choose a clear day.

## GETTING THERE

There is one **bus** a day from Los Cristianos and Playa de las Américas and one bus a day from Puerto de la Cruz. For most people, therefore, a **coach** excursion or a **hire car** will be the most appropriate way of getting there. It is possible to hire a **taxi**, but this will be an expensive way of seeing the park.

## GETTING AROUND

There is no public transport within the park, so if you do not wish to be at the mercy

of a coach driver, a hire car is the only option. Many people cycle around the park, although how they have the energy for this exercise after climbing 3000m (10,000ft) is a mystery!

## WHERE TO STAY

No camping is allowed within the Mount Teide National Park. The only formal accommodation option is at the **Parador Nacional de las Cañadas**, tel: 922 33 23 04, fax: 922 33 64 15. While this is an expensive option, it is in a marvellous setting and once the tour coaches have gone there is the mouth-watering prospect of watching the sun set on the snow-capped peak. Traditional Canarian food. **Log Cabins:** group accommodation is available in log cabins in the Mount Teide National Park near Arenas Negras. For information, contact the Ayuntamiento de Garachico, Plaza de la Libertad 1, E-38450, tel: 922 83 00 00, fax: 922 83 13 01.

## WHERE TO EAT

There is a restaurant and a snack bar at the Parador. There are also snack bars at

the upper and lower cable car stations. A number of popular restaurants are located around the Visitors' Centre at El Portillo. It is a good idea to bring your own picnic lunch as there are a number of purpose-built picnic sites both in and around the fringes of the national park.

## USEFUL CONTACTS

There are **Tourist Information Centres** at El Portillo at the eastern end of the park and also at the Parador. Both have information regarding whether hiking trails are open and the cable car is running. The government organization, **ICONA**, administers the park and they can be contacted on tel: 922 29 01 29.

**Cable Car**
It is important to check if the cable car is running. It can frequently close down because of wind, snow or maintenance. For more information, tel: 922 38 37 11.

**Travel Agencies**
The following travel agencies organize excursions to Mount Teide: Halcón Viajes, tel: 922 24 93 71; Viajes del Rosal, tel: 922 22 24 45.

# Travel Tips

## Tourist Information

The **Spanish Tourist Board** has offices in the USA (New York, Beverley Hills, Chicago, Miami), Canada (Toronto), Australia (Sydney) and several non-English speaking countries. In the UK, the address is: Spanish National Tourist Office, 22/23 Manchester Square, London W1M 5AP, tel: 020 7486 8077, fax: 020 7486 8034; 24-hour brochure request line: 0900 1669920; website: **www.tourspain.co.uk**

There are Tourist Board offices (ask for the *Oficina de Turismo*) on Tenerife in these towns:
**Santa Cruz**, Palacio Insular, Plaza de España, tel: 922 60 58 00; **Puerto de la Cruz**, Plaza de la Iglesia, tel: 922 38 60 00, fax: 38 47 69; **Playa de las Américas**, town centre, tel: 922 79 76 68, fax: 75 71 98; **Los Cristianos**, Town Hall, tel: 922 75 24 92, fax: 75 71 38; and **Reina Sofía Airport**, tel: 922 77 30 67. Staff usually speak English and provide brochures, timetables and help with car rental and accommodation.

## Entry Requirements

Visitors from Britain, Canada, USA, New Zealand and Australia must have a valid passport.

Those staying more than three months will require a visa from the Spanish embassy in their native country. Visa extensions on Tenerife must be applied for at the Gobierno Civil in Santa Cruz. Anyone arriving by ferry with their own car will need a driving licence and the international insurance Green Card.

## Customs

The duty-free allowance is: alcohol: one litre spirits, two litres fortified wine and two litres table wine; tobacco: 200 cigarettes or 50 cigars; perfume: 60cc (or 250cc toilet water); gifts: up to the value of £145.

## Health Requirements

No vaccinations are necessary unless coming from a country with smallpox, typhoid or yellow fever. There is no malaria and mosquitoes are rare. Visitors from EU countries should bring form E111 – this will gain them some degree of free medical treatment, but is no substitute for a good medical insurance.

## Getting There

**By Air:** Cheap charter flights go from many European countries direct to Tenerife. Scheduled flights (more expensive) go via Madrid. From North America, Australia and South Africa, the Madrid route is the only option. One of the cheapest scheduled services from the UK is the excellent Monarch Crown service from Luton (three times a week in winter and twice a week in summer). International flights arrive at Reina Sofía Airport in the south, which can be very busy at peak times. There are car-hire facilities. Taxis reach Playa de las Américas in about 20 minutes and Puerto de la Cruz in 1 hour 45 minutes. Regular buses run south to all the main resorts and north to Santa Cruz.

**By Ship:** The only ferry (for cars and foot passengers) from Europe to Tenerife comes from Cádiz on mainland Spain. It runs once a week to Santa Cruz and stops at Las Palmas in Gran Canaria en route. Book well in advance for summer sailings.

## What to Pack

With a mild climate year-round, there is no need to pack heavy clothing. A light jumper and windproof jacket are useful for evenings or trips to the mountains. For beach holidays, light sandals are recommended as the volcanic sand can become very hot underfoot. Stronger footwear is needed for hiking in the mountains. The sun can be strong all year, so sunglasses and sun hat are recommended. Light cotton clothes, shorts, swimming costumes and sun protection creams are essential for most holidaymakers. Ladies will find a sarong useful. Take smarter casual clothing for the evenings, particularly in hotels and expensive restaurants. Beachwear is unacceptable in churches. Canarians usually dress casually, except for formal occasions. Tenerife is highly photogenic and most visitors will bring a camera or camcorder. Spare films are readily available. If you should forget to pack an essential item, all is not lost. The tourist resorts have shops that sell clothing, beachwear, sports gear and books in various languages.

## Money Matters

**Currency:** The euro was introduced in January 2002. It is divided into 100 cents. Coins come in denominations of 1, 2, 5, 10, 20 and 50 cents. Notes are issued in 5, 10, 50, 100, 200 and 500 euros.

**Currency exchange:** Travellers' cheques and foreign currency can be cashed at banks, change outlets, post offices and hotels. Have your passport ready when cashing travellers' cheques.

**Banks:** Finding a bank is not a problem, although service may be slow. They are open on weekdays, 09:00–14:00; on Saturdays, 09:00–13:00. They will charge a small commission

cashing travellers' cheques, but will usually give a better rate of exchange than other places.

**Credit Cards:** The major credit cards are accepted throughout Tenerife in most shops, hotels, restaurants and exchange offices. There are automatic cash dispensers in the larger towns and resorts, in a variety of languages.

**Tipping:** A service charge is added to hotel and restaurant bills, so tipping is a matter of personal choice. A small gratuity can be paid for good service. Taxi drivers, guides and porters will expect a tip (*una propina*) of 5–10 per cent. There is no VAT in Tenerife, but there is a special Canary Island tax (IGIC) of 4½ per cent on retail goods and services, which will be included in all bills and prices.

## Accommodation

Most accommodation is geared to package tours, which means that the individual traveller who just turns up will usually find that the hotel or apartment is fully booked. It is best to book before arriving. There is a range of hotels from luxury five-star establishments to modest one-star pensions. Aparthotels have the usual facilities, but will have some self-catering rooms. State-run *paradores* are usually located in historic buildings, have traditional furniture and specialize in local food. Apartments far outnumber hotels and are usually cheaper. They normally have similar facilities (pools, bars, restaurants). Most apartments are self-catering, but a variety of food can be sampled in local restaurants. There are several official camp

---

| **PUBLIC HOLIDAYS** |
| --- |
| **1 January** • New Year's Day |
| **6 January** • Epiphany or Three Kings' Day |
| **19 March** • St Joseph's Day |
| **1 May** • Labour Day |
| **30 May** • Canary Islands Day |
| **25 July** • Feast of St James the Apostle |
| **15 August** • Assumption Day |
| **12 October** • Day of the Spanish Speaking World |
| **1 November** • All Saints' Day |
| **6 December** • Constitution Day |
| **8 December** • Feast of the Immaculate Conception |
| **25 December** • Christmas |

sites, mainly in nature reserves. To use them you need a permit. *Casas rurales* are converted farmhouses or village properties, an option for those wishing to get away from the bustle of the large resorts; advance booking is essential. Tenerife is a year-round destination, with a high season from December to March when the climate is attractive to northern Europeans. At this time of year the accommodation is at its most expensive and most likely to be fully booked. Summer is also busy; this is when mainland Spaniards come to Tenerife. Low-season prices for accommodation tend to be in May and November.

## Eating Out

**Restaurants** in the resort areas cater mainly for tourists and therefore generally provide international food. Usually there is a printed menu posted outside the premises, often with a national flag, and sometimes photographs of the food.

Fast-food restaurants abound, such as KFC, McDonalds and numerous pizza places. Food from Italy, Thailand, India, China, France and Mexico ensures a wide choice. For Canarian food, head inland or to the capital, Santa Cruz. Lunch rarely starts before 15:00 and the evening meal around 21:00 or even 22:00. However, in the resort areas, restaurants will be open for much of the day. Sample the many **fish restaurants** providing a variety of fresh shellfish (*mariscos*) and fish (*pescado*), usually at a reasonable price. **Cafés** and **bars** are everywhere and many provide tapas with the drinks. Cheapest is to order the meal of the day (*menú del día*), usually a starter, main course, pudding and drink.

## Transport

**Air:** Inter-island flights go from Tenerife to all the other Canary Islands. Most leave from Los Rodeos Airport in the north. Airlines include Binter, Spanair and Canarias Regional Air.
**Ferries:** All the islands are served by regular ferries, mostly Compañía Trasmediterranea or Lineas Fred Olsen.

**Buses:** Known as *guaguas*, buses provide a comprehensive service around the island. Most are run by the TITSA company and are green in colour. Bus stops (or *paradas*) are marked by a large sign with the letter P. Visitors should consider buying a Bonobus card, which gives a 25 per cent discount on tickets.
**Car Hire:** Rates are very reasonable and with a good, well-signposted road system, a car rental can add much to the enjoyment of a holiday. Most international rental firms have offices at the airport. Although in theory an International Driving Permit (IDP) is required, in practice most firms accept a valid national driving licence.
**Driving Hints:** In Tenerife you drive on the right, overtake on the left and give way on round-abouts to traffic coming from the right. Carry your driving licence and passport (or a photo-copy) when driving as the police can demand to see them. Seat belts should be worn at all times, including rear seats. It is prohibited to use a mobile phone when driving and to throw objects out of the car window. The blood alcohol

limit is 0.08 per cent and any driver involved in an accident can expect to be breathalyzed, so it is sensible not to drink alcohol if driving. Police can impose on-the-spot fines to non-resident drivers, but there is a 20 per cent discount if paid immediately. Visitors bringing their own car will need an IDP, car registration papers, a nationality sticker, a Green Card extension to the insurance policy and a red warning triangle in case of a breakdown. Speed limits are 120kph (75mph) on motorways, 100kph (70mph) on dual carriageways and 90kph (55mph) on other roads. The speed limit in built-up areas is 60kph (35mph). A motorway (*autopista*) runs two-thirds of the way around the island, from Playa de las Américas in the southwest to Puerto de la Cruz in the north. It is possible to drive all the way around Tenerife in a day. Progress on inland roads, however, can be slow, owing to rough surfaces and hairpin bends. Parking in the larger towns and cities can be difficult and it is best to use the underground car parks where provided. Pay and display areas are marked with blue lines. Cars parked illegally are quickly towed away and can be expensive, time-consuming and frustrating to recover. Breakdowns are usually caused by overheating – take spare water and oil on all longer journeys. It is illegal to tow one car behind another. In the event of an accident involving a hire car, report the incident to the hire firm immediately. Petrol stations are widespread and most accept credit cards.

| CONVERSION CHART | | |
|---|---|---|
| **FROM** | **TO** | **MULTIPLY BY** |
| Millimetres | Inches | 0.0394 |
| Metres | Yards | 1.0936 |
| Metres | Feet | 3.281 |
| Kilometres | Miles | 0.6214 |
| Square kilometres | Square miles | 0.386 |
| Hectares | Acres | 2.471 |
| Litres | Pints | 1.760 |
| Kilograms | Pounds | 2.205 |
| Tonnes | Tons | 0.984 |
| To convert Celsius to Fahrenheit: x 9 ÷ 5 + 32 | | |

Fuel is cheaper than in Spain and the rest of Europe. Tourist offices can provide adequate maps, but for more detail try bookshops. New Holland's Globetrotter Map of Tenerife is highly recommended.

**Taxis:** Tenerife's taxis are good value. They are generally white Mercedes showing a plate with the letters SP (*Servicio Público* – Public Service). For short journeys they are metered, but for longer journeys negotiate a fare with the driver. A green roof light indicates an available taxi.

**Trains:** There are no trains in the Canary Islands.

## Business Hours

Offices, post offices and most shops open 09:00–13:00. After the siesta period, they re-open from 15:00–19:00. Saturday opening is 09:00–13:00. Food stores and supermarkets may open for longer periods, while some shops in the tourist resorts may open on Sundays.

## Time Difference

Tenerife maintains GMT in the winter months, so there is a one-hour time difference with the continent. Clocks go back one hour during the summer.

## Communications

**Telephones:** The old three-figure regional digits have now been incorporated into the telephone numbers, so you have to dial all nine numbers even if phoning within the same town. For an international call, dial 00 and the country code, followed by the area code (omitting the first 0) and then the number. If dialling Tenerife from abroad,

the country code is 34, the same as the rest of Spain. There are many blue telephone booths, which take both phone cards and cash. Phone cards (*tarjetas telefónicas*) can be bought at post offices and tobacconists. For long-distance calls, the large cabins, or *locutorios*, are best. You pay at the desk on leaving and credit cards are accepted. Many cafés and bars also have public telephones, but these are more expensive than those on the street. The police emergency number is **091**. Visitors should have no difficulty using their mobile phones in Tenerife, as service providers automatically lock in to local suppliers.

**Post:** Post boxes are yellow. Stamps (*sellos*) are sold at post offices (*oficinas de correos*), newsagents and shops that sell postcards. Post offices open at normal office hours. The postal service is slow. Allow a week for a card to reach Europe, 10 days for North America and 14 days for Australia or New Zealand.

**Fax:** Most hotels will provide a fax service free of charge, but expect to pay a small charge for the service in a post office or tourist information centre.

## Electricity

The current in Tenerife is 220V, though some hotels have 110V sockets for shavers. Plugs have two round pins in line with most of Europe. Bring adapters for appliances as you will not be able to buy them in Tenerife.

## Weights and Measures

The metric system is used both in Tenerife and the rest of the Canary Islands.

---

### ROAD SIGNS

**Alto** • Stop
**Camino cerrado** •
Road closed
**Ceda el paso** • Give way
**Circunvalación** • Bypass
**Curva peligrosa** •
Dangerous bend
**Derecha** • Right
**Derecho** • Straight on
**Despacio** • Slow
**Derrumbes en la via** •
Rockfalls on the road
**Dirección unica** • One way
**Izquierdo** • Left
**No adelantar** •
No overtaking
**No estacionar** •
No parking
**No hay paso** • No entrance
**Peligro** • Danger
**Reduzca velocidad** •
Reduce speed
**Salida** • Exit
**Semáforo** • Traffic lights
**Trabajos en la via** •
Roadworks

---

## Health Services

Citizens of EU countries are entitled to free medical treatment on production of Form E111 (obtain before travelling). Form E111 does not, however, cover prescriptions or dental treatment and is no substitute for a good travel insurance policy covering medical treatment. Tenerife has five good hospitals and a host of private clinics. Hotels can usually provide the name of an English-speaking doctor (*médico*). For minor medical problems, go to a chemist (*farmacia*). Pharmacists in Spain give advice and are allowed to dispense a variety of prescription drugs. *Farmacias* are open during normal shop hours and are distinguished by an illuminated green cross. In a large town, at least one will be

### GOOD READING

**José Luis Concepción** (1984), *The Guanches – survivors and their descendents* (Ediciones Graficolor, La Laguna).

**Felipe Fernández-Armesto** (1982), *The Canary Islands After the Conquest* (Clarendon, Oxford).

**José Manuel Moreno** (1994), *Fauna of Tenerife* (Ediciones Turquesa, Santa Cruz).

**Lázaro Sánchez-Pinto and Lucas de Saá** (1993), *Flora of the Canary Islands* (Ediciones Turquesa, Santa Cruz).

**Ann and Larry Walker**, *Pleasures of the Canary Islands: Wine, Food, Beauty, Mystery.*

open after hours and a duty rota shown in the window. The Red Cross (*Cruz Roja*) often have small medical centres in kiosks on beaches in the main resorts. Services for **disabled travellers** are generally poor, particularly on public transport and in public toilets. The airport, larger hotels and many tourist attractions are more aware of wheelchair requirements. The resort of Los Cristianos has a very good reputation for wheelchair provision. It is advisable, however, to warn airlines and hotels of any special needs well in advance.

## Health Precautions

Visitors will experience few problems. Hygiene requirements are strict, so food poisoning is rare. The biggest danger is **sunburn** and **dehydration**. Use sun block, wear a hat and good sunglasses and avoid exposure during the hottest parts of the day. It is possible for the skin to be burnt even

when there is a layer of cloud. To avoid dehydration take plenty of non-alcoholic liquids. The main symptoms of heatstroke are nausea, headaches and increased heartbeats. Treat initially with rehydration solutions containing sugar, salt and water. Tap water in the main resorts is usually good, but less reliable in rural areas. The water is fine for brushing teeth, but bottled water (*agua mineral*) is advised for drinking. The fizzy version is *agua con gas* and the still variety *agua sin gas*. Another cause of illness is too much **alcohol**. Non-alcoholic beer (*cerveza sin alcohol*) is widely available, even on draught. There is no malaria in Tenerife, but mosquitoes and other biting **insects** can be a nuisance. Use insect repellent, especially in the evenings.

## Personal Safety

Crime is relatively low – the police keep a high profile. Most visitors will never feel threatened, but petty crime does exist, mainly bag snatching and theft from cars. Take a few simple precautions. Keep valuables in the hotel or apartment security boxes. Do not leave valuable articles in your car or take expensive belongings to the beach. Avoid badly lit areas at night. Keep cash in a body belt or pouch. Lock hotel windows and balconies. Beware of pickpockets in crowded places such as bus stations and markets. Keep photocopies of passports and driving licences. If you are the victim of a crime, report it to the police immediately and get a signed statement to present to your insurance company.

### USEFUL PHRASES

**Yes, No** • *Sí, No*
**Please, Thank you** • *Por favor, Gracias*
**Hello, Goodbye** • *Hola, Adiós*
**See you later** • *Hasta luego*
**My name is**… • *Me llamo…*
**Do you speak English?** • *¿Habla (usted) Inglés?*
**You're welcome** • *De nada*
**I don't speak Spanish** • *No hablo Español*
**How much is**…? • *¿Cuánto cuesta…?*
**Do you have**…? • *¿Tiene…?*
**Please speak more slowly** • *Hablé más despacio, por favor*
**Where is**? • *¿Dónde está?*
**What time does it arrive/ leave**? • *¿A qué hora llega/sale?*
**Do you have anything cheaper**? • *¿No tiene algo más barato?*
**Is there**…? • *¿Hay…?*
**Please fill the tank** • *Llénelo del todo, por favor*
**Is there a hotel near here**? • *¿Hay un hotel por aquí?*

## Emergencies

To contact the **police** call **091**. For **medical** emergencies requiring an ambulance call **062**.

## Etiquette

Topless sunbathing is a feature at beaches and pools, but full nudity is only tolerated at certain official locations. Beachwear is not acceptable when visiting churches and cathedrals.

## Language

The official language of Tenerife is **Castilian Spanish**, but the dialect is similar to that spoken in Andalucía or South America. English is widely spoken, particularly in the tourist industry.

# INDEX

Note: Numbers in **bold** indicate photographs